SECRETS TO START WHOLESALING REAL ESTATE TODAY

Books by John Lee

Secrets of a Deal'ionaire – Creating Wealth One Small Deal at a Time (2014)

Landlord Pennies to Banker Dollars (2019)

Secrets Those Credit Doctors Don't Want You to Know – Book and Workbook (2015, 2020)

4 Simple Steps to Prevent ID Theft and IRS Tax Refund Theft (2015)

How to Improve Your Credit Score – What Everyone Needs to Know (2010)

© HHLLC 2014, 2020. Secrets of a Deal'ionaire. Deal'ionaire OTC System Premier Signature Series. All Rights Reserved.

SECRETS TO START WHOLESALING REAL ESTATE TODAY

3 SIMPLE STEPS TO SCREAMING DEALS

© HHLLC 2014, 2020. Secrets of a Deal'ionaire. Deal'ionaire OTC System Premier Signature Series. All Rights Reserved.

SECRETS TO START WHOLESALING REAL ESTATE TODAY

3 SIMPLE STEPS TO SCREAMING DEALS

© HHLLC 2014, 2020. Secrets of a Deal'ionaire. Deal'ionaire OTC System Premier Signature Series. All Rights Reserved.

This information may not be reproduced, copied, stored in a retrieval system, recorded by video, audio, scanned, photographed, transmitted in whole or part, in any form by any means, electronic, mechanical, photocopying, recording or otherwise shared in any way whatsoever without written permission of the owner under penalty of law and remains the sole property of the owner.

This information is intended for illustration purposes only. Actual financial impact may vary as it may be affected by additional factors not considered in this information. The results generated by the strategies, methods, or techniques described in this information should not be used for any planning, forecasting or any other similar business purposes.

The information is provided "AS IS" without warranty of any kind, express or implied, and in no event shall the owner be liable for any damages whatsoever in relation with the use of this information. The participant agrees to indemnify and hold harmless and waive any liabilities or claims against the owner that result from this information.

Confidential — Non-Transferable Licensed Material © 2014, 2020 HHLLC. Secrets of a Deal'ionaire. Deal'ionaire OTC System Premier Signature Series. All Rights Reserved.

SECRETS TO START WHOLESALING REAL ESTATE TODAY

3 SIMPLE STEPS TO SCREAMING DEALS

By

John Lee

© HHLLC 2014, 2020. Secrets of a Deal'ionaire. Deal'ionaire OTC System Premier Signature Series. All Rights Reserved.

Acknowledgement and Dedication

This book was written for all of you who would like to get into real estate investing without *Breaking the Bank*.

With the internet and technology, many real estate "Gurus" have arisen. Many of these so-called Gurus have never done a real estate deal. Some have done just a few. And some just took enough training to get a TV show.

There are many popular TV shows today that make real estate investing look fun and appealing. It seems like anyone can make money in this arena.

We all can enjoy watching a program while dreaming of making more money than we do at our jobs. And all we have to do is *flip-this-house*. Who doesn't want to live in Hawaii and make tens of thousands of dollars every few weeks?

There are people out there who want to sell you a high-priced course or seminar for several thousand dollars. Some are selling expensive mentorship programs for tens of thousands of dollars (and more) and preying on unsuspecting newbies.

There are others still who start real estate groups with the intention of selling you their properties as *good deals*. Many of these properties are *not* good deals and are difficult for them to sell as retail properties or as investments to other investors.

Don't get me wrong. There are many Gurus who *do* have a good heart and *do* want to teach you for the right reasons. You just have to sift through the garbage to find them.

My intention is to help you get started without all of the confusion that some like to cloud you with. Real estate is not as complicated as many would like you to believe.

The real fact is, you *can* make a lot of money investing in real estate. And it's not by forking your hard-earned cash over to one of those Gurus.

You will become successful investing in real estate through education. Applied education, that is. Simply learn all you can, pick out a strategy, and put it into practice.

Most real estate investors start out with wholesaling strategies. You do not need money or credit of your own to do this. Most of us continue to do wholesale deals, even if we invest through other techniques.

Like anything else that succeeds, real estate investing a team sport. It takes a strong team to win the World Series. You may become the MVP, but rarely will you win a game without the help and efforts of the other members of your team.

It also takes a team to write a book and share your knowledge with others. These pages would not be here without the MVPs on my team.

There are so many people who helped me to get to this point, and I would like to recognize a few.

As usual my wife, Laura, has helped me with her honesty — sometimes her brutal honesty. Laura can and will set me straight even when I think things should be said *differently*. She is seldom wrong, and I am always better off listening to her. My drummer does not always have the right beat like hers does.

My brilliant editor, Meg Stefanac has again made the words flow so well that even I can understand them. What I may think is easy to say does not always make sense until Meg gets done crafting it.

The cover is never complete until Brenda Hite does her magic. I attempted to make a book cover on my own once — keyword: *once*. And yes, it looked like I did it. Never again. Brenda has a way with designs and colors for covers that only she can create.

There are so many real-estate giants who have taught me along my own journey and have encouraged me and helped me along the way.

I am indebted to my mentor and friend, five-time *New York Times* best-selling author Robert G. Allen. Bob wrote the foreword for the first book in the *Secrets of a Deal'ionaire* series.

Also, I give thanks to AJ Rassamni, my dear friend and an excellent businessman, who has pushed me forward when I really needed it.

Lastly, Jennifer Hammond, host of *The Jennifer Hammond Show* on SiriusXM channel 126. Jennifer has always inspired me to share with others. She has a way of doing for others what they cannot always do for themselves.

These are just a few of the MVPs on my team. There are many others, but there's not enough time or room to mention them all. Most of you know who you are. I graciously say *Thank You!*

The information that is contained in these pages is for all of you out there who would like to get into real estate *without* breaking the bank.

You truly can make $5,000 to $10,000 in 30 days with No Cash, No Credit and No Problem.

John Lee

Table of Contents

Acknowledgement and Dedication......................ix

INTRODUCTION..1

- Step 1- What Are Screaming Deals for You?......5

1. What if You Have Absolutely NO Cash, NO Credit & NO Clue What to Do?...............................7

2. What Is This Wholesaling You Speak Of? 13

3. What Kinds of Screaming Deals Are You Looking For? 19

- Step 2 - Where Do You Find Screaming Deals?... 31

4. Where Do You Find These Screaming Deals at Such a Significant Discount? 33

 - Step 3 - What Do You Do with These Screaming Deals? 51

5. You Got a Screaming Deal - Now What? 53

6. Where Are These Cash Buyers that Will Buy My Screaming Deals in 30 Days? 75

7. Is Wholesaling Really This Simple?..................93

8. Special Bonuses Just for You! 101

9. Now You Are Ready to Follow These 3 Simple Steps Today!..113

HAAs 125

Real Estate Investing Strategies 129

Real Estate Math - Intentions 133

Real Estate Jargon 135

Real Estate Websites... 209

Property Checklist 212

SECRETS TO START WHOLESALING REAL ESTATE TODAY

INTRODUCTION

Everything in this book is for you. It's the basics of wholesaling real estate for the beginner. It also contains a few nuggets for the veterans.

You have surely heard the phrase "practice makes perfect." This is true when it comes to real estate wholesaling as well, so be sure to practice as you hone your skills.

One of my mentors, T. Harv Eker, has a different take on the practice makes perfect saying. He says, "practice makes permanent." You must work on your craft to perfect it. Rarely does someone *make it* overnight. It usually takes years of practice to become an *overnight success.*

Practice is actually the art of perpetuating your habits, whether good or not-so-good. Since you are going to form habits anyway, why not form good ones?

There are many opportunities in this world to create wealth. Real estate just happens to be the best, in my opinion. With today's technology and all of the resources we have, I believe everyone who wants to, deserves to enjoy at least a little piece of the real estate pie.

Wholesaling real estate is probably the easiest strategy of any to make fast cash. You only need to know some basics to get started. You can change your life and well-being in just a few short weeks.

With the information I am sharing here, you can get started today. What are you waiting for? Let's do it now!

- Step 1 -
What Are Screaming Deals for You?

1. What if You Have Absolutely NO Cash, NO Credit & NO Clue What to Do?

Chapter 1

What if You Have Absolutely NO Cash, NO Credit & NO Clue What to Do?

"Being broke is not a disgrace, it is only a catastrophe." ~ Rex Stout ~

So, You're Broke and Know Nothing. That's Okay.

There's a big difference between being broke and being poor. Being broke is a current situation. Being poor is a mindset.

Okay, so you're broke. I get it. Very few of us are born with a silver spoon in our mouth or get to live a life in which we don't have to think about money and survival.

It seems that about every five to seven years, we tend to face a major life change. These changes are often unexpected and have the potential to cause financial distress.

We may go through a bad divorce (ever heard of a good one?), have an unexpected death in our family, be hit with unmanageable medical bills, welcome unexpected new additions to our households, or encounter other circumstances we hadn't necessarily planned for.

Life changes aren't the only things that can cause us to have financial troubles. Maybe you're in a dead-end job. Or maybe you love your job, but it just doesn't pay enough to cover your bills.

It's possible that you're one of the lucky ones who have a good job and a comfortable lifestyle, but you just want to have more. You might want a better car or a bigger house. You might want to take nicer vacations. You might want to be able to build financial security for future generations.

Whatever your reasons for needing and wanting more money, wholesaling can provide it for you.

In my case, I simply did not want to work so hard being a mortgage broker. That is why I got into the investment side of real estate. And when it comes to real estate investing, wholesaling is one of the best ways to get a seat on lucrative side of the table.

What if You're New to this and You Know Absolutely Nothing?

So, you want to get started but you don't have a clue about what to do. That's okay. Many times, it's best to start with nothing and from nothing. That way, you have nothing to lose—including bad habits.

What you will learn here is how you can make $5,000 to $10,000 (or more!) in 30 days with NO Cash, NO Credit, and NO Problem.

Wait a minute... Don't you need to have good credit to invest in real estate? Surprise! No, you don't.

You might be saying, "My credit is so bad, I couldn't borrow enough for an Uber ride home."

You might be under the misconception that you need to have a high credit score in order to be able to invest in real estate. This is actually not true. You do not need to have good credit to get in on the wholesale real estate game.

You could have recently had a property foreclosed on or could have just gone through a bankruptcy. You could have the worst credit on the planet.

It doesn't matter.

Wholesaling is one of the most forgiving forms of real estate investing. Even better, you *cannot* lose money if you do it right.

Wholesaling is by far the best way to get into real estate or to add to your arsenal if you are already an investor.

It is the ideal vehicle to enable you to make thousands of dollars in the next 30 days, no matter what your current financial situation is.

What is This Wholesaling You Speak Of?

2. What Is This Wholesaling You Speak Of?

Chapter 2

What Is This Wholesaling You Speak Of?

"The most complicated skill is to be simple." ~ Dejan Stojanovic ~

But Isn't Real Estate Investing Complicated & Risky?

Let's get one thing straight right off the bat: Wholesaling is **not** complicated, and it's **not** risky.

In fact, it's probably the simplest and least risky method of all real estate investing options.

Wholesaling is a strategy through which an average person can become an investor simply by putting a property under contract and then selling that contract, or paper, to another investor at a profit.

Yes, it really is that simple.

With just a little knowledge, you'll be able to make thousands of dollars in just a few weeks. You read that right, a few *weeks*.

How is Wholesaling Actually Done?

Real estate wholesaling is a simple process. It just involves finding a house that can be bought for a price that is well below market value, analyzing an approximation of the cost of repairs, putting the property under contract, and selling it to a rehabber (usually someone who fixes-and-flips or buys-and-holds property).

"Wait," you may be thinking. "I don't know anything about finding a discounted house, estimating repairs, or filling out a contract and then selling the house!"

Exactly. That's why you're reading this simple to follow process. So, you will know. It's probably the easiest business you will ever learn. You'll see.

We are going to go through the very simple, easy-to-follow steps that anyone can learn. There are just a few things you need to know to get you started.

With just a little bit of knowledge you will be wholesaling like a pro in no time.

In a very short time, you will know:

The 3 Simple Steps to Wholesaling.

1. What Are Screaming Deals for You
2. Where Do You Find Screaming Deals
3. What Do You Do with These Screaming Deals

And...

Most Important...

-How to Make $5,000 to $10,000 in 30 days with NO Cash, NO Credit & NO Problem!

So, by now you are probably thinking, "I cannot wait!" Me, too. Let's get started.

What Kinds of Screaming Deals Are You Looking For?

3. What Kinds of Screaming Deals Are You Looking For?

Chapter 3

What Kinds of Screaming Deals Are You Looking For?

"The way to find a needle in a haystack is to sit down." ~ Beryl Markham ~

We Must Find a Deal at a Significant Discount

We are looking for houses that we can buy at a significant discount. We want at least 65% to 70% off of the retail price. That is, *after* repair costs or after repair value (ARV) and *after* your fee, which is typically $5,000 to $10,000.

So, we are looking for houses that can be bought for a lot less than most of the ones that are listed for sale by a typical real estate agent.

Of course, not all real estate agents are typical, some are also investors.

How Will You Know if This is Really a Screaming Deal?

Home values can be challenging to estimate. Houses, just like anything else, are worth whatever someone else is willing to pay you for it.

I'm an amateur coin collector. I have pennies that I have paid a couple thousand dollars for. Yes, a couple of *thousand* dollars. These pennies still have a legal tender value of one cent. I could take one out today and spend it. So are these pennies worth a cent, or are they worth thousands of dollars?

Property values work in a similar way. Houses are worth whatever someone is willing to give you for them. There are a couple of ways to get a rough estimate.

I use the term, *rough estimate* here because that's what it is. You will get better as you go along. Usually at first it is a *guestimate*.

Your guestimate is much like Zillow's *zestimate*. Zillow gives home values for the addresses they have in their database. This is not an appraisal and there are many factors not considered by Zillow's zestimate.

You will never really know the *true* retail value of what a property is worth. But you **can** get a good idea in a couple of ways.

The closest you can probably come to a good guess is by looking at the properties that have sold in the area in the last six months. The homes you will want to look at are those that are similar in style and square footage.

Look at the sales prices of homes that are:
- of like construction (i.e. brick or frame)
- of similar size (within 200 square foot of living space)
- located in the same zip code, within two miles, and not crossing a major street.

These are just general guidelines and are certainly not carved in stone. There are other factors you can consider, but many times you can throw all these other factors out of the window.

A good place to start is by looking on the county website. Many show information regarding previous home sales—but some do not.

There are also some real estate sites that show their *estimates* of property values. Google the address of the property you are considering, and it will usually give you a few sites to look at. This will get you started. Again, the values are not carved in stone.

You can usually get a more accurate value by consulting a real estate agent. This works best if you are lucky enough to have a friend in the business. Most real estate agents will not be willing to waste their time looking up previous sales in the area when you are not going to buy a house from them.

Let's face it, would you want to waste your time giving away your expertise to someone who will not be doing business with you? I think not.

The closest property-value estimate would come from an appraiser. This is what the banks use to make loans on properties. But we will not be spending hundreds of dollars for an appraisal. It is not necessary and is still a subjective number.

Your end buyer will have a very good idea of what they think the property is worth. That is all that really matters to us wholesalers anyway. And when you have a screaming deal, it will be scarfed up quickly.

Make Sure to Include Your Profit

Let's use a $100,000 retail price for an example to make it easy. To make a quick deal, we will want to sell the property for about 70% of its value, or, in this case, for $70,000.

If the house needs $10,000 in repairs and we want to make $5,000 in profit, we would need to pay no more than $55,000 for it. If we want a $10,000 profit, we cannot pay more than $50,000.

You might be wondering why we would want to sell the property for $70,000 when it is worth $100,000.

Simply put, the end buyer, whether they're a rehabber, reseller, fix-and-flipper, or a buy-and-hold landlord, will need to have enough room for their profit. There also has to be enough wiggle room for dealing with the *unknowns.*

The unknowns are usually in the repair estimates. The $10,000 that was originally *guestimated* in repairs, can very easily turn into $20,000 or more.

For example, a torn down wall may reveal previous water damage that necessitates replacing the studs as well as the drywall.

There may be electrical system that seemed fine at first glance but that actually need to have the circuit box and most of the wires replaced.

There may be unforeseen plumbing issue or some kind of roof and eave issue that needs to be addressed. The unknowns can pop up all kinds of places including decks, patios, basements, kitchens and bathrooms.

Even experts can miss things when estimating repairs costs. Even if the homeowner tells you everything they know about the property—and they usually don't—there are still many unknowns.

And then there are the unexpected *surprises* that code enforcement inspectors will almost certainly come up with.

Simply put, there's no possible way to know the exact amount that repairs will eventually cost you. Instead, you need to rely on estimates.

You will get better at making estimates the longer you are involved in wholesaling. When you are first starting out, don't get too worried. Ask the sellers what they know about the property. Then look at the house yourself.

Look for the obvious. Do the windows look old? Do the faucets work and look ok? Are there leaky pipes? What about the lights? Does the electric box look like it's been updated? Are there still old-time fuses in the panel?

Is the kitchen outdated? What about the bathroom? You do not have to be an expert to see if the home has had any updates in the last thirty years.

When you're new at this, how do you know what the repairs will actually cost? You will never know exactly. You will just need to make a guestimate.

Take lots of notes and call some experts. You can call a window company and ask them how much new windows will cost, installed. Same with the roof and anything else that you think will need to be repaired.

At first, you can base your costs on calls to people who do the type of work that will be needed. After you see the same repairs a few times, however, you will become good at guessing what the repair costs without the need for making inquiries.

You will also have your potential buyers looking at the house before they buy it, and they will give you their opinions and guestimates. They will all have different ideas of what needs to be repaired and what the cost will be.

Fix-and-flip resellers will have different repairs and cost than those who buy-and-hold. In a short time, you will come to understand what is important to each type of buyer.

So how do you know if you actually have a screaming deal? Very simply, when you have a good deal, the property will sell very quickly. If you do *not* have a buyer right away, you do not usually have a good deal.

Once you are known as someone that finds good deals, the buyers will come out of the woodwork. The easiest part of this business is finding the buyers.

There are so many rehabbers, resellers and buy-and-hold buyers out there. And the serious buyers have money. Yes, there are many, many cash buyers. And that is how you are going to buy these properties, all cash.

You are essentially a cash buyer when you are a wholesaler. But, *you do not need cash of your own*. Without using any of your own money, you will be offering cash to your sellers. That is their motivation for selling their properties to you at a significant discount.

So what exactly are we are looking for? A house that we can buy for 65 to 70 cents on the dollar. The price we pay is after repair cost and *our* profit. Remember, you do not have to be an expert at estimating repairs. You will get better over time.

Now that you know what you are looking for, let's look at **where** to find these deals. They are not just sitting on a shelf waiting for us come by and fill our shopping cart.

The kinds of houses you are looking for are typically not going to be listed by a real estate agent or a realtor. And they are not going to be

listed on the *MLS*. (The MLS is the *Multiple Listing Service* that is used by real estate agents.)
The properties on realtor websites and the MLS are usually retail properties with no room for profit for investors.

Most of the houses that make good deals will actually be bought directly from owners themselves. However, it is important to keep in mind that many of the *FSBO*s (For Sale by Owner properties) are **not** screaming deals.

We'll look at where to find screaming deals in the next section.

Where Do You Find These Screaming Deals at Such a Significant Discount?

- Step 2 -
Where Do You Find Screaming Deals?

4. Where Do You Find These Screaming Deals at Such a Significant Discount?

Chapter 4

Where Do You Find These Screaming Deals at Such a Significant Discount?

"Minds are like flowers, they only open when the time is right."
~ Stephen Richards ~

Why Would Anyone Sell Their Home for Less than They can Get with a Real Estate Agent?

Although many will tell you that finding good deals is the hardest part of wholesaling, I say, "Not really."

There are many places you can find these properties. They are all around us. Once you start to identify them, you will see that they are everywhere.

Most of the homes you are looking for are not listed with a real estate agent or a realtor. They are not listed on the MLS. Many aren't listed anywhere at all.

In fact, a real estate agent would not *want* to list most of the houses we are looking for. Most need too many repairs and the sellers cannot or will not put the money into making these repairs.

There are many reasons *why* someone will sell their property at a discount:

- There are divorces that involve a court order to sell the home.
- There are deaths. Many times, the heirs live out of town, making it a hassle to fix up the property to retail condition.
- Elderly homeowners often move into assisted living facilities. Sometimes they cannot or will not fix up their homes to a retail condition.
- Sometimes good people find themselves in difficult situations and just want to unload the house without putting money into it. As I said before, we all seem to have some sort of a major life change about every 5 to 7 years.

These are all cases where the homeowners simply cannot or will not spend the money, time and resources needed to fix the properties up to a retail condition.

That's where we come in.

And remember: The amount of profit these houses can offer usually goes up as the condition of the property goes down.

Where Are These Houses?

There are so many ways to find screaming deals, and I recommend using multiple methods. We'll look at a few of the easiest, though there are many more.

Getting started is as easy as opening up your computer or smart phone. You don't even have to leave your couch.

This is something you can do just about any time. Even for those of you that have full-time jobs and a family to care for. What about you stay-at-home moms or those with disabilities? Yes, you can do it too.

Surfing for Dollars

I like to call this method "Surfing for Dollars." We'll talk about driving for dollars, talking for dollars, and walking for dollars in a bit. Let's start with surfing the internet.

We have so much access to information these days. There are a number of useful websites we can use, such as Craigslist and Zillow.

Look for houses that are posted for sale *without* a real estate agent. There are a few key words and phrases you'll want to look out for.

FSBOs

You should be on the lookout for FSBO, or "For Sale by Owner."

Not all FSBOs are homes that can be obtained at a discount. Many times, property owners opt to sell their home on their own in order avoid paying the real estate agent commission.

This commission can be substantial. Depending on the agent, the commissions can be as high as 6% or 7%. On a $200,000 house that can be as much as $14,000!

This may seem like a lot of money to give to someone just for listing and showing your house to potential buyers. On the other hand, it may be well worth the cost if you have a very good agent who can sell your house quickly at a great price.

What you want to look for are FSBOs that are being sold without a real estate agent mainly because no agent will agree to list the home. This is typically because the house needs too many repairs, which the seller cannot or will not fix. Most retail buyers are not in the home repair business and are not looking for screaming deals.

In other cases, the property owners may be upside down on their home loans. That is, they owe more to the bank than they can sell their home for. In this case there may not be enough room to tack on a real estate agent commission.

Most houses that are upside-down do not have enough room for us wholesalers either. Remember, we need to get a substantial discount that includes repair costs and our profit.

There are other ways to solve the problem of upside-down home loans. There are short-sale specialists that do that. Short sales are not for us wholesalers. That is another strategy altogether.

Fixer-Uppers and Handyman Specials

Be on the lookout for properties advertised as "fixer-uppers" and "handyman specials."

Look also for other key words and phrases like "needs work," "must sell," and "Attention investors!"

Be aware that not all of the ads that use these terms are what we are looking for. Some are great deals, but many are not.

Some ads are also from other wholesalers. They are running ads like the ones you will posting. Keep in mind that it is a good way to meet others in the business.

Run Your Own Ads

Post your own ads. Many places today let you post ads for free. Keep your ads simple and right to the point. Most people skim things these days and will not read through a lengthy ad.

Simply say something like, "We Buy Houses! Any Area, Any Condition! We Pay Cash and Can Close in 30 Days." Keep your ads this simple.

Driving for Dollars

Another good way to find deals is through a method I call "Driving for Dollars." This involves driving through various neighborhoods and looking for homes that appear empty or abandoned.

This can be done in your own neighborhood or any other area. Look for things like grass that needs to be cut or snow that hasn't been shoveled from the driveway or walkways.

Look for newspapers collecting on the lawn. Another good sign of an empty house is mail accumulating in the mailbox.

There could potentially be boarded up windows, depending on the neighborhood and situation. Maybe there are broken windows.

Talk to the neighbors. When you see someone working in their yard, go over and introduce yourself. Tell them you are an investor who is working in their neighborhood.

People generally do not like to have run down homes nearby their own, so they'll usually be happy to meet you.

Often, these neighbors have been in their homes a long time. They care about their neighborhood. Many know the history of the houses on their street. They'll know who's lived in the house in question, for how long, and if there was a change in the family, even the story of their dogs.

In fact, some neighbors like to talk so much you may be there all afternoon. You might find out more than you ever cared to know. Sometimes you'll wish you had taken a potty break before you walked over there. Ha-ha, not kidding at all.

Talking for Dollars

Tell your friends and family members that you buy houses. You are an investor. You do not have to tell them exactly what you do and how you do it. But you do want to tell them.

The people you know frequently know other people who need to sell their homes. Get the word out so others know what you do. You may end up with a few great leads this way.

Get some business cards made up that say *We Buy Houses*. Put your phone number and email address on the cards. I like to include my name on the cards as well. You don't really have to though. You can put a company name instead.

When you talk to the potential sellers, ask questions like Why are they selling? How long have they owned the home? What repairs are needed?

Sellers love to tell you their story. Listen to them. Tell them you are there to solve their problem. Because, let's face it, they have a problem.

Their problem is they need to sell their home for some reason. Find out their reason and solve their problem.

Walking for Dollars

I know a few people who like to walk for exercise. Some stay within their neighborhoods, and some walk quite a distance. Some of them look for empty homes while they are walking. They are looking for either themselves or for me.

If you are Walking for Dollars, look for the same indications you look for when you are Driving for Dollars.

The signs of an empty house are usually there and since you are moving slower than when you are driving, you might catch things you may have otherwise missed.

Being Creative for Dollars

There are several more ways to find screaming deals. One of my favorites is to ask the letter carriers. The people who deliver our mail usually know the homes in the neighborhoods very well.

The letter carriers know the houses where the mail is accumulating and not being picked up. They may not want to tell you the exact house numbers, but they may be able to point you in the right direction.

You can offer them, as well as others, a finder's fee for locating the houses that you end up buying.

Most people, even non-investors, like to make a little extra cash.

Bandit Signs

Bandit signs can be a good way to find screaming deals. These are those signs that you see on the side of the road and at intersections that say, *We Buy Houses.*

These signs can be a great source for finding potential sellers. The signs are very inexpensive. You can get them from a local printer or buy them online.

The first set of bandit signs I bought, I found online. I don't remember the exact site, but it offered something like 50 signs for $89. They also gave me an additional ten free signs if I agreed to put out five signs advertising their business.

Of course, I put their signs out. I just put them out by mine. In fact, when I first started putting out bandit signs, I would only put them next to other signs.

It actually turned out to be a good idea to put my signs out by others. I figured that if other signs were there, it must be a good spot. It turns out that most of the time, it was.

You can also buy signs that can be attached to the side of your vehicle. You've no doubt seen them. Many are magnetized so they can be removed easily.

There are some places you might go that you would prefer not to have signs on your vehicle. Magnets make it easy to take them off.

Bandit Sign Cautions!

Many municipalities have ordinances that forbid the posting of bandit signs. Some forbid signs of any kind. It is up to you to familiarize yourself with the laws and ordinances in the locations where you may want to post signs.

I lived on a busy street a few years ago and it was a great place for posting signs since there was a lot of traffic. I probably got five to ten calls a week from my signs.

Then, suddenly, my signs started disappearing. As I pulled up to my house one day, I saw a real estate agent taking down one of my signs. It just so happened that the house next door was for sale, and I guess the agent thought my signs were a threat to his sale.

So, I got a ladder out and put my sign high on a telephone pole that was between our houses. I also took some clear grease and put it around the edges. That way, if anyone tried to remove my sign, they would get grease on their hands.

The sign remained in place just fine for a couple of weeks. Then one day, I was standing in front of my house talking with a friend of mine, when an official city public works truck pulled up.

A worker got out and removed a ladder from the back of his truck. He climbed up the ladder and proceeded to remove my sign from the pole.

And yes, he got the clear grease on his hands — and also on his nice polo shirt with the official city logo on it.

He was not very happy. He proceeded to say a few colorful words under his breath. I acted like I didn't notice while my friend was chuckling.

That was the last sign I put on the pole. Since then, the city passed an ordinance forbidding signs of any type.

At that same time, I had a small truck that I parked in front of the house. What I started doing was putting signs in the front and rear windows when I parked the truck.

No one messed with my signs and they were legal as far as the city was concerned. Best of all, I still got a lot of calls from my signs.

Many municipalities now charge you fines for posting illegal bandit signs. Some fines are as high as $600 per sign! I've heard of investors being summoned to court for having posted dozens of signs.

I'm not sure what the outcome was for their court appearances, and I don't think I want to know. Don't let this be you!

Another Bandit Sign Caution

One day, I was talking to my insurance broker. He just happens to be a real estate investor also. (Most of the professionals I do business with are investors themselves. I like dealing with investors since we tend to have a different mindset than those who don't invest.)

My broker advised me *not* to put signs on the side of my truck while driving. I would not be covered for liability reasons in the event of an accident. I would need to list my vehicle as a commercial vehicle in order to be covered.

My insurance would, however, cover damages to my vehicle as long as the truck was parked while the signs were attached. I just needed to remove them when operating the vehicle.

Check with your insurance company or representative *before* driving around with signs on your vehicle. It's usually best to avoid a problem rather than to deal with the aftermath if a problem arises.

Bird Dogs

Many of us wholesalers hire what we call *bird dogs.*

You can offer bird dogs $500 to $1,000 (or whatever amount you want) if they find you an empty home that may be for sale. Tell them it cannot be a property that is currently listed with a real estate agent.

You can also tell your friends and family that you will give them a finder's fee when they refer a home that you end up buying. Be sure to make it clear that you must buy the home in order for them to collect the fee.

Start Finding Your Screaming Deals!

There are many other places where you can find screaming deals. I just shared a few of the easiest to help you get started. Following these few suggestions should get the screaming deals for you with *NO CASH, NO CREDIT and NO PROBLEM.*

Next we'll go over what to do once you find a screaming deal.

You Got a Screaming Deal – Now What?

- Step 3 -
What Do You Do with These Screaming Deals?

5. You Got a Screaming Deal - Now What?

Chapter 5

You Got a Screaming Deal – Now What?

"Fog and smog should not be confused and are easily separated by color."
~ Chuck Jones ~

Don't You Need a Real Estate License? And Isn't the Paperwork Complicated?

Many people will tell you that you need to have a real estate license to engage in wholesale real estate transactions. And, many people are wrong.

You do **not** need a real estate license in order to be a wholesaler. In fact, you don't need **any** kind of professional license to be a wholesaler.

I am not an attorney, so please do not consider this legal advice. Check your state laws for any variations. My experience has taught me that there are things you must do the right way.

Do the right thing and do not deceive anyone. Make sure that the deals you make are win/win/win.

Don't You Need a Company to Buy and Sell Real Estate?

No. Your first few deals will probably be done using your name as the buyer.

Eventually you'll want to form an entity, i.e. a company such as an LLC or corporation. There are different types of companies you can set up. The one that is right for you will depend on your particular circumstances.

You can check with your attorney or accountant for help determining which is best for you. In the state where I live, it only costs around $50 to start and register an LLC (Limited Liability Company).

I recommend doing your deals using an entity. This is because an entity can put a buffer between your personal assets and your company assets. Every situation is different, of course, so you'll want to go with whatever works best for your circumstances.

You don't need to set up an entity right away. You may need to make money as soon as possible and may therefore want to get started immediately. In most cases it is alright to just do business using your own name.

When I first got started in this business, I did my work using my name. After doing a few deals, I formed an LLC. The first one I formed was done with the help of my attorney. Since then, I have formed a few additional LLCs on my own.

You May Know Nothing About Contracts. What Do You Need to Know?

Once you and the seller come to an agreement on a price, you'll need to get the property under contract. This is not difficult. You only need a couple of pieces of paper.

Yes, you heard me right. You only need a couple of pieces of paper.

You will need a sales contract transferring the property from the seller to you. And you'll need an assignment form to transfer it from you to your end-buyer.

You simply tell the seller that you or one of your partners will be buying their house. You want to make sure you tell them this, so there is no confusion down the road.

More than likely, someone else will be bringing the money and taking title to their property. You are acting as a wholesaler, not the bank or the one supplying the funds.

This has never been a concern for any seller I have ever entered into a contract with. They just want to sell their property and really don't care where the money comes from.

So, it doesn't really matter whether your first few deals are done using your name as the buyer, or an LLC/company.

There are also a couple of clauses you will want to put in the contract.

What Clauses Should You Put in the Contract to Protect Yourself?

There are a couple of clauses you should include in the contract in order to protect yourself and let the other party know what you are doing. These clauses can protect you from problems related to any potential misunderstandings.

Assignment Clause

You are going to want to include an *assignment clause*. This simply states very clearly that the seller is transferring the property to you (as the buyer) *and/or assigns*.

It's very simple. Just make sure you have it included in your Sales Agreement contract.

This clause tells the seller that they are selling the property to you and/or another entity (or partner). No one has ever questioned this. As long as they get the agreed upon amount of money, it can come from anywhere.

Exit Clause

The other clause you must have in your contract is the clause that allows you to walk away from the deal. This is necessary in the event you totally screwed up and cannot sell the property.

There are only a few things that would cause you to back out. One is if you were way off on your estimate for the cost of repairs. Another is if there is a title issue that cannot be fixed. For these reasons, and not many more, you may not be able to sell the property.

In these instances, you need to be able to walk away from the deal without being obligated to fulfill the contract, i.e. getting stuck buying the property yourself.

The exit clause you must include in every contract simply states: ***Subject to Inspections and/or approval of partners.*** That's it.

By including these two simple clauses you make it possible to:
- assign the contract to another entity, and
- walk away from the deal for any reason.

The Contracts

As for the paperwork, it only consists of two simple forms. All you need is a one-page **Sales Contract** and a one-page **Assignment Form.** I also carry a five-page sales contract with me just in case.

Although I have never used it, I have heard that there are some sellers who are more comfortable with a contract that looks like a standard realtor's contract. A standard contract may be several pages long.

Be aware that in most states, only a licensed real estate agent can use a standardized contract that is state-approved. We, as wholesalers, are not required to use such contracts. I do carry one though, just in case anyone would ever happen to prefer one.

You'll probably want to carry some blank contracts with you at all times. You never know when you are going to run into a deal. It's really nice to be prepared right there on the spot.

In the past I have hand-written contracts on blank pieces of paper, and more than once, I've done it on a napkin. Nowadays, I almost always have the appropriate paperwork with me.

So, what do these simple one-page forms consist of? Here is a sample of the one-page Sales Contract and Assignment Form. I'm also including a multi-page contract for illustrative purposes.

One Page Sales Contract with Seller

CONTRACT TO PURCHASE REAL ESTATE

BE IT KNOWN, the undersigned _____ and/or Assigns (Buyer), offers to purchase from _____ (Owner), real estate known as _____

City/Town of _____, County of _____, State of _____, said property more particularly described as:

The purchase price offered is $ _____ **CASH**

Deposit herewith paid	$ _____
Balance at closing	$ _____
Total:	$ _____
	CASH

This contract is conditional upon the following terms:

1. This contract is for purchase of said property in "as is" condition.

2. This contract is subject to Buyer's approval and Buyer's partner's approval, in writing, of a walkthrough inspection of said property prior to closing.

3. Said property is to be sold free and clear of all encumbrances, by good and marketable title, with full possession to said property available to Buyer at date of closing.

4. The closing shall occur on or before _____ at the office of Buyer's escrow agent, unless such other time and place shall be agreed upon.

5. Other terms:

Signed this _____ day of _____, 2020.

Buyer _____ Date _____

Buyer _____ Date _____

Seller _____ Date _____

Seller _____ Date _____

Sample of Multiple Page Contract with Seller

AGREEMENT FOR SALE

THIS AGREEMENT OF SALE made this _____, 20__, between **Heartland Hideaways LLC** and/or assigns (PURCHASER) and _____ (SELLER)
WITNESSETH:

1. DEPOSIT. That for and in consideration of the sum of **Heartland Hideaways** LLC in the form of
(Cash $_____) (Check $_____) (Check $_____) (Note $_____) which of due and payable on
_____, 20__, receipt of which is hereby acknowledged by AGENT, the PURCHASER agrees to buy and the SELLER agrees to sell all that certain piece, parcel or lot of land with all improvements thereon, described as follows:

2. PROPERTY DESCRIPTION. (Street Address)
_____
Legal Description: **list by closing agent**

3. CHATTELS AND/OR EQUIPMENT. Included in the sale price, existing built-in heating plants, existing air conditioning systems, plumbing and lighting fixtures. **Legal Description of the Property etc.**

4. PRICE AND FINANCING.
$_____ TOTAL PURCHASE PRICE of which
$_____ shall be paid in cash, certified or cashier's check at settlement, the above deposit to be a part thereof. $_____ shall be paid by proceeds of a First Deed of Trust or First Mortgage loan (Assumption, these figures are approximate. PURCHASER is to (Place) (Assume) a (Fixed Rate.) (Adjustable Rate every (year) (month) (Conventional) (FHA) (VA) (FIRST DEED OF TRUST OR FIRST MORTGAGE LOAN BEARING INTEREST AT THE (Fixed) (Initial Adj.) RATE OF _____% PER ANNUM OR THE PREVAILING RATE AT THE TIME OF SETTLEMENT. IN THE CASE OF VA FHA (MCDO), PURCHASER AGREES TO PAY THE MAXIMUM PERMISSIBLE INTEREST RATE AT SETTLEMENT. LOAN TO BE REPAYABLE $_____ PER MONTH APPROXIMATELY, INCLUDING PRINCIPAL AND INTEREST (Taxes, Hazard Insurance, PMI or monthly FHA insurance, if any, to be additional.) WITH FHA/VA FINANCING, AND WHEN PERMITTED, PAYMENT OF THE TOTAL FHA INSURANCE PREMIUM OR VA FUNDING FEE OF APPROXIMATELY $_____
IS TO BE FINANCED BY THE PURCHASER AND ADDED TO THE LOAN AMOUNT NOT $25,000.00 approximately, shall be paid by proceeds of a second (commercial) (seller held) DEED OF TRUST OR MORTGAGE) bearing interest at the rate of _____% per annum, payable at $_____ per month approximately, said payment to be applied first to interest, with remainder applied to principal, and due and payable in full _____ years after settlement date hereof. If subject Property is transferred, sold or conveyed, or any interest therein is transferred, sold or conveyed, the note and deed of trust shall be due and payable in full unless the transfer, sale or conveyance is consented to in writing by the current noteholder. This note may be paid in full or in part at any time without penalty. A late payment fee of $_____ will be charged for any payment not received by the noteholder within _____ days of the due date. Default on the first trust shall operate as a default on the second trust (or hereinafter) lender for disbursement of such loan by settlement. SELLER shall have _____ ( ) hours after delivery of the PURCHASER'S financial data to approve or reject the credit-worthiness or request additional information regarding PURCHASER's credit-worthiness. In the event SELLER has not approved PURCHASER's credit-worthiness in writing within _____ ( ) hours of the last request for information, this Contract shall be null and void and the deposit returned to the PURCHASER upon execution of appropriate release documents. $5,000.00 Other financing See ADDENDUM.
LOAN FEES: BASED ON THE FINANCING TERMS SPECIFIED HEREIN, THE PURCHASER SHALL PAY UP TO THE FIRST _____ OF THE TOTAL LENDER POINTS (INCLUDING LOAN ORIGINATION, LOAN DISCOUNT AND BUYDOWN FEES). THEREAFTER THE SELLER SHALL PAY THE NEXT _____ OF THE TOTAL LENDER POINTS AND THEREAFTER THE PURCHASER SHALL PAY THE REMAINDER OF THE TOTAL POINTS. THE PURCHASER IS TO PAY THE

INITIAL PMI INSURANCE (IF ANY), VA FUNDING FEE (IF ANY), LOAN ASSUMPTION FEE (IF ANY), AND ANY OTHER ALLOWABLE CHARGES MADE BY LENDER.

5. BALLOON PAYMENTS. PURCHASER acknowledges that the loans, if any, described herein or by addenda hereto may require substantial lump-sum (balloon) payments on the due dates thereof, and PURCHASER further acknowledges that neither the SELLER nor the AGENT has made any representations regarding the future availability of mortgage money, or interest rates thereon, for the refinancing of any such lump-sum payment when due.

6. OTHER TERMS.

Subject to Inspections and/or approval of partners.

_____

_____

_____

7. SETTLEMENT DATE. TIME IS OF THE ESSENCE. The SELLER and PURCHASER agree to make full settlement in accordance with the terms hereof on, or with mutual consent, before the _____, 200_. If a longer time is required to secure a report of the title and a survey, or to finance or process the loan, if applied for in accordance with this Contract, then, the date of settlement shall be extended the sufficient time to effect these conditions.

8. SETTLEMENT AGENT. PURCHASER makes it known that he desires to employ _____ as Settlement Agency. _____.

9. AGENT'S FEE. SELLER agrees to pay AGENT compensation on the sale price of the Property as agreed upon between SELLER and listing broker. The party making settlement is hereby irrevocably authorized and directed to deduct the brokerage fee from the proceeds of the sale and disburse _____ of the purchase price as compensation to $_____ as listing broker.

10. V.A. FINANCING. It is expressly agreed that, notwithstanding any other provision of this Contract, the PURCHASER shall not incur penalty by forfeiture of earnest money or otherwise be obligated to complete the purchase of the Property described herein, if the Contract purchase price or cost exceeds the reasonable value of the Property established by the Veterans Administration. The PURCHASER shall, however, have the privilege and option of proceeding with the consummation of this Contract without regard to the amount of the reasonable value established by the Veterans Administration. PURCHASER agrees that should PURCHASER elect to complete the purchase at an amount in excess of the reasonable value established by V.A. PURCHASER shall pay such excess amount in cash from a source which PURCHASER agrees to disclose to the VA and which PURCHASER represents will not be borrowed funds except as approved by VA.

11. FHA FINANCING. It is expressly agreed that, notwithstanding any other provision of this Contract, the PURCHASER shall not be obligated to complete the purchase of the Property described herein, or to incur any penalty by forfeiture of earnest money deposit or otherwise, unless the SELLER has delivered to the PURCHASER a written statement issued by the Federal Housing Commissioner setting forth the appraised value of the Property (excluding closing costs) of not less than _, which statement the SELLER hereby agrees to deliver to the PURCHASER promptly after such appraisal value statement is made available to the SELLER. The PURCHASER shall, however, have the privilege and option of proceeding with the consummation of this Contract without regard to the amount of the appraisal valuation made by the Federal Housing Commissioner.

12. POSSESSION DATE. Unless otherwise agreed to in writing between the principals hereto, the SELLER agrees to give possession of said premises at the time of settlement. If the SELLER fails to do so and occupies said Property beyond the time of settlement, SELLER shall become and be thereafter treated by sufferance of PURCHASER and hereby expressly waives all notice to quit as provided by law. PURCHASER shall have the right to proceed forthwith by any means available to recover possession of said premises.

13. LOAN APPLICATION. PURCHASER agrees to make written loan application within five (5) business days following ratification of contract. If PURCHASER's loan application is rejected, for reasons other than appraised value, and with SELLER approval, the PURCHASER will make application to one additional qualified lender in order to obtain the aforesaid financing. Failure of PURCHASER to diligently pursue loan procurement shall be considered a default, and SELLER may avail himself of all legal and equitable remedies. If new financing is to be arranged, or if assumption of existing financing requires lender approval, then this Contract is contingent upon such new financing or approval upon the terms herein described. Any assumption fees or costs shall be at PURCHASER's sole expense. If said financing or approval cannot be obtained, this agreement shall become null and void, the deposit refunded in full to the PURCHASER, and all parties released from any further liability hereunder, upon execution of appropriate release documents.

14. EQUIPMENT, CONDITION and INSPECTION. PURCHASER accepts Property in its present physical condition except as otherwise provided herein. Appliances, heating and cooling equipment, plumbing and electrical systems and smoke detectors will be in working order at time of settlement or PURCHASER's occupancy, whichever occurs first. SELLER agrees to deliver the Property free of trash and in broom clean condition and grants to PURCHASER or his representative the right to make a pre-occupancy or pre-settlement inspection.

15. WELL & SEPTIC. If Property is on well and/or septic systems, SELLER agrees to furnish PURCHASER on or before settlement with a certificate from the appropriate government authority, or licensed or reputable private company, indicating that the well water is potable and the septic system is functioning satisfactorily and meets design criteria and capacity requirements of the appropriate authority. If either system is found defective, or substandard, SELLER will take appropriate remedial action at his expense.

16. TERMITE INSPECTION. At settlement, SELLER is to furnish a report from a properly licensed pest control firm showing subject house and any other dwelling and/or garage(s) within the Property lines (excluding fences or shrubs, not abutting dwelling(s) or garage) to be free of visible termite and other wood destroying insects and/or visible damage therefrom. Required extermination and repairs from current and/or prior infestation shall be at SELLER's expense.

17. REPAIRS. If as a condition of providing the financing called for in this Contract, the Lender requires repairs to be made to the Property, the SELLER will notify AGENT in writing whether or not he will make the repairs. Should SELLER elect not to make repairs, the PURCHASER will notify AGENT in writing whether or not he will proceed to settlement pursuant to this Contract without the SELLER completing the repairs. All decisions must be made within five (5) days of receipt of notice from AGENT. If neither SELLER nor PURCHASER agrees to make the repairs, then this Contract will become null and void. This clause will not release the SELLER from any responsibilities specifically written into the "Other Terms" paragraph nor paragraphs 14, 15 or 16 hereof or any terms specifically agreed to in any addendum to this Contract.

18. DAMAGE OR LOSS. The risk of loss or damages to said Property by fire, act of God, or other casualty remains with SELLER until the execution and delivery of the Deed of Conveyance, and recordation thereof.

19. PURCHASER COVENANTS. Mortgagee at time of settlement, PURCHASER shall have in force, and keep in effect, hazard insurance equal to at least the aggregate of the principal balance(s) of all deed of trust notes on the subject Property, naming the lender(s) thereof as additional insured's.

20. PRORATIONS. Rents, taxes, water and sewer charges, fuel oil, homeowner association dues and/or condominium fees (if any) and any other operating charges are to be adjusted to date of settlement. Taxes, general and special, are to be adjusted according to the certificate of taxes issued by the collector of taxes, if any charge that recorded assessments for improvements completed prior to the date of ratification hereof, whether assessments therefore have been levied or not, shall be paid by the SELLER or otherwise made therefor at time of settlement. If Deed of Trust(s) is assumed, interest shall be adjusted to the date of settlement and PURCHASER shall reimburse SELLER for existing escrow accounts, if any.

21. TITLE. The Property, including the aforesaid utensils and/or equipment, shall be sold free of encumbrances except as aforesaid. All notices of violations of orders or requirements of any county or local authority, or actions in any court on account thereof, against or affecting the Property at the date of settlement of this Contract shall be complied with by the SELLER and the Property conveyed free thereof. Title is to be good and marketable subject to easements, covenants, conditions and restrictions of record, if any, otherwise the deposit is to be returned and Contract voided at the option of the PURCHASER, unless the defects are of such character that they may be remedied by legal action within a reasonable time, but the SELLER and AGENT are hereby expressly released from all liability for damages by reason of any defect in the title. In case legal steps are necessary to perfect the title, such action must be taken promptly by the SELLER at his own expense, whereupon the time herein specified for full settlement by the PURCHASER will be extended as specified in Paragraph 7 hereof. If SELLER refuses to settle according to the terms herein, for any reason, the costs incurred for the title examination, appraisal, survey and the real estate commission as set forth shall become due and payable immediately by SELLER.

22. FEES. Fees for the preparation of the Deed of Conveyance, Grantor's Tax, appropriate legal fees and any other proper charges assessed to him shall be borne by SELLER. Fees for examination of title (except as heretofore provided), recording charges (including those for any purchase money trust), appropriate legal fees, loan assumption fees and costs attendant to the assumption of the existing financing, and any other proper charges assessed to him shall be borne by PURCHASER.

23. DEPOSIT. The earnest deposit shall be held by AGENT in a special escrow account until settlement, to conform with the Virginia Real Estate Board Regulations and/or as required by the Veterans Administration Section 1806, Title 38, U.S. Code. PURCHASER acknowledges that the earnest money deposit is placed in AGENT's escrow account, paid on all of which is placed on no interest bearing account from time to time, and waives claim to any interest resulting from such deposit. If the PURCHASER shall fail to make full settlement, the deposit herein provided for may be forfeited at the option of the SELLER, and/or AGENT, or the SELLER may avail himself of other legal and equitable remedies. In the event of forfeiture the deposit will be divided equally between SELLER and AGENT. (AGENT's share of any forfeiture shall not exceed the amount of compensation due under the terms of the Contract) Settlement is to be made by the office of the Settlement Agency or the Title Company searching the title. Deposit within the Settlement Agency of the cash payment as aforesaid, the executed Deed of Conveyance and such other papers as are required of either party by the terms of this Contract shall be considered good and sufficient tender of performance of the terms thereof.

24. AGENT DISCLOSURE. AGENT hereby discloses that AGENT may from time to time engage in the general insurance business, title insurance business, mortgage loan business, real estate settlement business and other real estate related businesses and services. Therefore, in addition to AGENT's compensation specified herein, AGENT may receive fees related to other services provided in the course of this transaction.

25. TYPEWRITTEN OR HANDWRITTEN PROVISIONS. Typewritten or handwritten provisions included in this Contract shall control all printed provisions in conflict therewith.

26. ASSIGNABILITY. This Contract may be assigned with the consent of the PURCHASER.

27. CONVEYANCE. SELLER agrees to furnish and convey the above Property by General Warranty Deed with usual English covenants of title, the same to be prepared at the expense of the SELLER.

28. AGENCY. UNLESS OTHERWISE DISCLOSED IN WRITING, PARTIES ACKNOWLEDGE THAT THE SELLER, NOT THE PURCHASER, IS REGARDED AS THE AGENT'S CLIENT. HOWEVER, AGENTS WHO ARE REALTORS ARE OBLIGATED TO TREAT FAIRLY ALL PARTIES TO THE TRANSACTION.

29. COVENANT. The parties to this agreement agree that it shall be binding upon them, and each of their respective heirs, executors, administrators, successors and assigns, that the provisions hereof shall survive the execution and delivery of the Deed aforesaid and shall not be merged therein, that this Contract, unless amended in writing, contains the final agreement between the parties hereto and that they shall not be bound by any terms, conditions, and statements, warranties or otherwise.

_____ _____

_____ _____
Buyer(s)   Seller(s)

_____ _____
Date   Date

One Page Assignment Contract with Buyer

Assignment of Contract

_____Heartland Hideaways LLC____ *Assign's to*
Branden Hurley & Tamara Gazillion *the contract on*
(address) _3717 Lady, St Louis MO 63114_____

Between_____Robert & Julia Maynard_and _Heartland Hideaways LLC___
Dated _December 13, 2020_.

The contract is being assigned for the sum of _$5000___
Paid upon closing at closing.

Total sales Price including Contract & Assignments is $30000_ plus closing cost.

Assignee_____ Date _____

Buyer_____ Date _____

Buyer_____ Date _____

Tips to Help Make Your Deal go Smoothly

Three tips from me to you:

>1. Make sure you have an extra copy of the sales contract so you can leave one with your seller. Be sure that both copies are signed. That keeps everything on the *up and up*.
>
>2. Tell the seller that you will be closing in 30 days and that you will be having some of your partners coming by do some inspections during this time.
>
>3. Let the seller know that you will be putting a lockbox on their house and will need a key. In the event that they or someone else is currently occupying the home, you will call first.

Sometimes the seller may have a brother-in-law, a child, or some other family member living in the house to keep it from being empty. Make some kind of arrangement with the occupants to ensure that you have access to the property.

Your potential buyers will want and need access in order to make sure they actually want to buy the property. This is not usually a problem since the sellers typically want to sell their home, and very quickly.

A lockbox can be picked up at almost any hardware or big box store for just a few bucks. Most sellers are fine with you having access to their home when no one else is there.

Now, What Do You Do with These Pieces of Paper?

Now that you have the ball rolling, the next step is to send your paperwork to a title company. Do this immediately. They will do the background checks on the title for you.

The title company will check for liens and a number of other things that may affect and/or cloud the title.

When a title is *clouded*, most of the time it needs to be cleared before it can be transferred.

There could be others who must sign over their rights before the seller can legally transfer the property.

There could be a *mechanic's lien*. This happens when a previous contractor who has done work on the home has not been paid and has placed a lien on the property. It is possible that the contractor has since been paid but has not yet released the lien.

There could be heirs who are involved, due to a previous owner's passing. What if the previous owner died and cannot sign? There are affidavits for this.

There could be *encumbrances*. An encumbrance is the right to, interest in, or legal liability on real property that does not prohibit passing title to the property but may diminish its value. It includes things like electric poles on the property where the power company has the right to enter the property for service.

The title company can also find *appurtenances*. Appurtenances are accessories, rights or a privilege associated with a property. It could be as simple as furnaces, window dressings, or outbuildings.

Almost anything that may accompany the principle property can be an appurtenance. Many are written into the contracts themselves.

So, You Don't Know Anything About Titles. Aren't They Complicated?

Don't worry. It's not your job as a wholesaler to know anything about titles.

Yes, titles can be complicated. But that's a title examiners job. They will go through the process of examining the title for transfer for you.

The end-buyer will usually buy title insurance from the title company. This insures that in case the title company happened to miss something, the insurance would pay the cost to remedy the problem.

No worries on your part. Don't get wrapped up in trying to understand something that's not your concern. If there's something you need to do, such as get the seller to find someone who needs to sign, they will tell you.

Where Do You Find a Title Company?

There are a few ways to find a *wholesaling-friendly* title company.

The best way is by talking with members of a local REIA (*Real Estate Investment Association*) group. There are many local REIA groups. They can be found in just about every city or county. Most are full of experienced investors who can recommend investor-friendly title companies in the area.

You can also simply pick up the phone and call title companies near you. Tell them you have a property under contract and will be assigning it to another buyer.

Most title companies know the wholesaling process and will tell you upfront if they are wholesaling-friendly. If not, move on. There are so many that do these deals every day.

You could also ask your end-buyer what title companies they like to use. End-buyers often have a lot of experience in the wholesaling process and, if so, are likely to have a title company they prefer to work with.

Your end-buyers love to have people like you finding them screaming deals on properties. Whether they are a fix-and-flip or a buy-and-hold investor, they usually cannot find all the deals on their own.

So, that is the simple process of what to do with the few papers you have when you have a deal.

Ok, it sounds easy. But you may be saying, "I need cash *now*! Where are these *cash buyers* who are waiting to buy this screaming deal from me within 30 days?"

Finding them is a lot easier than most people think.

Where Are These Cash Buyers that Will Buy My Screaming Deals in 30 Days?

6. Where Are These Cash Buyers that Will Buy My Screaming Deals in 30 Days?

Chapter 6

Where Are These Cash Buyers that Will Buy My Screaming Deal in 30 Days?

"Sometimes I'm confused by what I think is really obvious. But what I think is really obvious obviously isn't obvious."
~ Michael Stipe ~

Isn't it Hard to Find Cash Buyers?

Many people will tell you that you must get your buyers list together before you start looking for deals. They'll say that finding buyers is the hardest part of wholesaling.

I actually think it's the easiest part.

There are so many cash buyers out there today. Right now, seems to be a seller's market. When you have a screaming deal, buyers come out of the woodwork.

This is also the way to know whether or not you actually have a good deal. You should have a buyer in less than a week. If not, you probably are not looking at a screaming deal.

And remember, if you're not actually holding onto a great deal, you have an escape clause in your contract. I personally have never backed out of a deal. But it's a good stress reliever to know that you can walk away if you made a mistake.

Get Leads through Local REIA Groups

One of the best places to start looking for buyers is at your local REIA group. This is where many like-minded investors gather, usually once a month, to share ideas and deals.

It's also a great place to learn techniques and market tips, as well as what is going on locally. REIA groups are a great source of information.

There are big differences in the types of groups that are out there. Most of the groups you'll find today are *for-profit* REIAs. There's nothing wrong with making a profit. We all have to make money and that's why most of us are dabbling in real estate.

Just make sure to find out where they are making their money and what the group's motivations are.

Are they bringing in local and national speakers who are selling a course, seminar, books, trainings or a weekend bootcamp? Or are they personally trying to sell you a coaching or mentorship for tens of thousands of dollars?

Many REIA groups in my area are charging those who don't know any better $40,000 to $50,000 for a one-year mentorship. They look for unknowing newbies, and they do find a few.

If you have an extra $50,000 lying around and want to give it to someone for information that costs no more than a few dollars, go ahead. If not, be wary. There are plenty of folks out there who want to sell you bridges!

Don't get me wrong. Mentors can be very good to have and can save you years on your road to success. Just make sure you know what you're getting into and what your options are.

Some groups get together every month so they can try to sell you their properties that are *really* hard for them to sell. They will say things like, "These are *off-market* deals and not on the MLS!" In reality, they cannot easily sell these properties as retail or even to other investors.

There are still a few *not-for-profit* REIA groups out there. Here in my city, we are fortunate to still have one. STLREIA is the oldest and still "**The**" not-for-profit REIA in St. Louis.

You should expect to pay dues when you join an REIA. Even those of us who are board members pay the same dues as all the other members. As of right now, the dues are only $75 a year for two people living at the same address.

The board members work on a volunteer basis, but they do get a few perks such as a little behind-the-scenes information and conversations with some well-known national real estate investment trainers.

The not-for-profit REIAs are generally more about education. They are more about the well-being of their members. I personally like to help educate people *without breaking the bank.*

That is why I'm sharing this information with you in this book. I don't want you to break the bank learning something that is easily learned.

Sometimes I joke, saying I'm probably the only person you know who has spent more than $150,000 on education and still does not have a degree.

The real joke is, that was back in 2010. Since then, my wife, Laura, and I have and traveled all over the world to attend educational seminars, trainings and camps. The difference is, we know what we are spending for.

Is it worth spending a lot of money on education and self-improvement? To me, yes. Just make sure you know what you are getting into. When you are just starting out, I caution you, "Learn as much as you can *WITHOUT BREAKING the BANK!*"

Regardless of what kind of REIA you are attending, there are usually a networking sessions or times designated to allow you to network with the other members and guests.

Find out what others are doing. Exchange business cards with them. Or just collect theirs if you do not have any. You should at least have some that say *We Buy Houses* like we talked about earlier.

There's a wealth of information at REIA meetings and you will almost always learn something from being around investors who have the right mindset. I go to at least two meetings a month as well as to lunches and meetup groups.

There's always something of value to learn. Never think that you know it all. Many of the people I learn from these days are a lot younger than I am.

Of course, the basics tend to remain the same in real estate. There is really nothing new. There are just different ways of doing things and different techniques.

By networking with other investors, you will find out about new trends and learn new ways of doing things and implementing strategies.

REIAs are also a great place for finding your prospective buyers. Find out who the buyers are. Find out who is doing fix-and-flips and who is doing buy-and-holds. There are many players in this arena.

These investors often attend local REIA meetings and are always on the lookout for screaming deals. Once you give them one of your screaming deals, they will come back looking for more.

Run Your Own Ads

Just like you looked through ads to find the screaming deals, you can place ads to find buyers. Other investors are constantly combing through the ads looking for screaming deals.

It doesn't take much, and it's not hard to write an attractive ad. You just need an enticing headline. Make it short with some key words.

Use words and phrases like:
- FSBO
- Attention Investors
- Handyman Special
- As Is
- Needs Work
- Fixer-Upper
- Must Sell!

There are many other attractive headlines you can also use.

Look through the ads and see what grabs your attention. Feel free to *borrow* what others use in their headlines. These are not copyrighted and there are some very creative marketers out there.

Remember that nothing is really new. There are just different ways of saying and doing things. Even the emojis that are used now are not new. The Egyptians used hieroglyphs thousands of years ago. Those were their emojis. Today, we just might add a smiley face and a heart instead of a bird and a snake.

Keep the body of your ad short and sweet. People skim ads these days and will not read every word, unless it is brief.

Let's face it. We are all limited with our and can only waste so much of it. I read recently that we are exposed to about 5,000 marketing ads every day. That's a lot of chaos!

So, keep your ads brief and to the point. Tell your target audience things like how many bedrooms and baths are in the house. Put in garage info like, attached, detached, one-car, two-car, carport, etc. Include amenities the home may have.

I never put the exact address of the property in my ads. I usually put something like 12XXX Main Street. I make them call for more info so I can make sure it's a real person.

Say it needs work but don't give too many specifics. Instead, say *Call for More Details*. And they usually will. Don't worry. The people who are looking buy houses that need work, will not usually take up a lot of your time.

Unlike the sellers who tend to want you to tell you their complete life story, including why they are selling the house, your potential buyers just want to know the facts.

You'll have better results if you actually answer your phone when you run your ads. Many people today would rather get a voice-mail message or an email. I get it. With all of the scammers and robo-dialers out there, we don't want to waste our time or get scammed.

While potential buyers *will* usually leave a message for you, most sellers will not. It's probably more important to answer your phone when you are buying than when you are selling.

Either way, however, you will almost certainly have better results when you actually answer your phone when it rings.

Bandit Signs & Vehicle Signs

You know those bandit signs and vehicle signs you used when you were looking to buy houses? Look for signs posted by other people. These signs can be a great source for finding potential end-buyers. And these buyers seem to be everywhere once you start looking for them.

Many people say they never really noticed them until they start looking for them. And once they started looking, they were amazed by how many there actually were out there.

The people who advertise *We Buy Houses*, usually really do buy houses. Just like you, they are looking for screaming deals. Call them. Put them on your buyers list.

Yes, do start a buyers list. You do not have to have one when you first start out, but you do want to get around to making one. That way, you will have a list of investors who are hungry for your screaming deals. These investors will be happy to be on your list and to be one of your *go to* people.

What Do You Say to These Potential Buyers?

When talking to your prospective buyers, keep it simple and right to the point. Tell them that you have a house under contract, and you are going to assign, or sell, the contract.

These buyers will know what you are talking about. They know they will be paying you for the opportunity that you have brought to them with this screaming deal. And they will be more than happy to pay you.

What Stops the Buyers from Going Directly to the Sellers and Cutting You Out?

The buyers cannot go directly to the sellers because you already have a contract with the seller. You have the exclusive right to assign or sell your contract to another entity. Period.

I have never had a buyer try to go behind my back and attempt to buy a property that I already had under contract directly from the seller.

I guess it *could* happen. That would be someone who you would not want to do business with. That person will have a very short career in this environment. Investors talk.

You've got to remember that most of your buyers are in the business for the long haul. If they would even remotely hint on cheating you out of a deal, that would probably be one of the last deals for them.

Investors are looking to build a relationship with you. They will want you to be one of their *go to* guys (or gals!). They want to be able to come back to you over and over for all of the screaming deals you will be able to offer them.

Should You Tell Your Buyers How Much Money You're Making?

Do the buyers get upset because you're making $5,000 to $10,000 profit? In my experience, no. They are happy to give you five to ten thousand dollars for a screaming deal.

Most of the time, they are going to be able to make a lot more money on this screaming deal than you are. If they are a *fix-and-flip* investor they are usually going to sell the property at retail price.

In most cases, your end-buyers will have a large profit margin.

When the deal is figured right, there is a nice spread left. Even if there are some errors in calculations or some unforeseen repairs, there's still a good margin left for profit.

You will not always know the exact amount needed for repairs and updates. Plus, there are almost always a few unknown and unforeseen factors. This is the main reason why it is usually best to start off your real estate investing career as a wholesaler.

Add Your $5,000 to $10,000

This is where your assignment contract comes into play. It states plainly the amount of your contract from the seller and the amount you are assigning or selling the contract for.

The generally agreed-upon amount that you should tack on for your contract fee is between $5,000 and $10,000 dollars. Sometimes more, sometimes less. You might find a really great screaming deal and make more. On the other hand, the deal you found might be just so-so, and in that case you'd take less.

Keep in mind, you are acting as a problem solver and you are therefore there to solve problems. The seller has a problem. They need to sell. The buyer has a problem. They want to buy. Your problem is to make money while solving theirs.

Everyone has a problem, and you're their solution-person. The more deals you do, the easier it will be to make sure everyone walks away happy. Some deals, you will simply have to walk away from because you can't provide the results the others are looking for.

Your assignment contract will be sent to the title company where you also send your sales contract. The title company you deal with will know the process.

Your fee will be right on the HUD settlement statement. It will have you listed as one of the payees of the proceeds.

This is usually the best way to do transactions. It ensures that everyone is on the same page as far as where the money is coming from and where it is going to.

You may wonder what the seller will be thinking about you making five or ten thousand bucks off this deal. It's never come up with any transaction I have done. Usually, the sellers are just happy to get rid of this *albatross*.

There *are* ways to close transactions that do not reveal your profit. Some people teach and like to do *double closings*. This hides the amount of money you are making.

A double closing is where you have one contract with the seller going to you. You have a separate contract going from you to the buyer. It is actually two separate deals. You are on title for a short period of time.

Some people prefer to do this when they are making a large amount of money on a deal, such as $50,000 or $100,000 or more! They think their buyer will not be happy to see them profit this much.

There are title companies that will do these double-closing types of transactions, but not everywhere. These transactions are actually illegal in some states.

As with any real estate transaction, it's best to know your state and local laws. I personally do not look good in stripes or orange jumpsuits with numbers on the back. I don't do double closings.

I have found that it's always best to let everyone know everything up front and to be open and honest about what you are doing. It's never cost me a deal, and investors *do* continue to contact me looking for more screaming deals.

By following this very simple technique, you will have $5,000 to $10,000 in 30 days.

Is Wholesaling Really This Simple?

Screaming Deals Are as Simple as 1, 2, 3

7. Is Wholesaling Really This Simple?

Chapter 7

Is Wholesaling Really This Simple?

"If you want to be successful, it's just this simple. Know what you are doing. Love what you are doing. And believe in what you are doing." ~ Will Rogers ~

Simply Be a Problem Solver, and You Will Be Successful!

The right attitude in this business will get you everywhere. Trust me; if you are in this for the right reasons, you will do very well.

At first, many turn to real estate investment as a way to make some quick money.

I see people coming into this business because they need money yesterday. Some folks wait until they are desperate or destitute and then scramble for ways to make ends meet. This may be you. If so, don't worry.

At some point in our lives, we have all faced situations where we have had a very short deadline to come up with a good bit of much-needed cash. That's the nice thing about wholesaling. We can turn deals into cash in weeks instead of months or years.

You can make $5,000 to $10,000 in 30 days with No Cash, No Credit and No Problem. As you have learned, money does exchange hands. It's just not *your* money.

You just want a small piece of that money. Yes, five to ten thousand dollars may be a lot of money to you…so far. In the big picture, however, it is but a drop in the bucket. So why not fill your bucket with lots of those drops?

Who knows? After getting a few drops in your bucket, you may want to become a fix-and-flip or a buy-and-hold investor. You may want to get into commercial deals, land speculation, note buying and selling, or even creating your own notes like I do.

Note creation is something I am very passionate about. I go more in depth on this topic in a couple of my other books including *Landlord Pennies to Banker Dollars*.

Regardless of what you eventually end up doing, you are most likely going to continue wholesaling. Most of do — even when we are actively engaging in another type of investing.

The longer you are in the business, the more deals and opportunities will come your way. You cannot, and will not, handle all of the screaming deals yourself. You will most likely hand off some of these deals to partners and acquaintances.

It has never hurt me once to pass off a screaming deal and make a few bucks by helping someone else.

Yes, I'm constantly on the lookout for ways to solve someone else's problems, but I rarely look for these screaming deals today. They just come to me. People know me as the go-to guy who knows how to solve problems and make deals work.

That's what you want to be: a problem solver. That's really what this business is all about, solving problems for others.

The seller has a problem, the buyer has a problem and we have a problem. There's rarely a real estate problem that cannot be solved in a way that makes all three parties happy. The problems that continue to go unsolved are usually that way only because of limited thinking.

There are many naysayers out there who will point out many reasons that something cannot be done successfully. And for them, that may be true. I've found that whatever you believe is true becomes true for you.

Rarely have I ever run into a problem that did not have some kind of solution. When it comes to real estate, there is not much that *can't* be done.

"Can't" simply means you do not know how or do not want to do something. It may not be the way you want to do it or the way you think it should be done, there is a way to get it done.

Do It for the Right Reasons

I go into every situation with the attitude that everyone must win.

It must be a win/win/win, or I will not do the deal. I cannot stress this enough: it's best to be honest upfront and do things the right way.

Sure, you will run into deals that you may be able to fudge on or not completely tell the whole story about so you can make a few extra bucks. This can be especially tempting when you are just starting out and desperately need cash now.

Don't do it.

You have your whole career, and lifetime for that matter, to build and create your reputation. Do not ruin yourself right out of the gate over one small deal. What you may think is insignificant could turn out to be a major bombshell to someone else.

It is never worth being known as *that guy*. The person who cannot really be trusted. And don't get into deals with anyone like that either. Always remember what Dr. Phil says, "If they'll do it *with* you, they'll do it *to* you!"

You want to be known as the person who can get things done. The one who does things the right way. The good guy. The Problem Solver.
I always try to do things as though I am doing them on stage in front of the whole world.

What if everyone were watching? What would they think of me? Would my Mom be proud of what I am doing? Not just okay with it, but **proud**?

As you progress in your wholesaling business, you will meet others who feel the same way. These are the people who will become your friends and business partners.

Folks who do things the right way are the people you will want to share deals with, and they are the people you will want to have sharing deals with you.

Become known as someone who can be trusted and the go-to person that others want to do business with. Make your reputation a good one and the deals will come to you.

You'll be glad you did.

I Have a Couple of Special Bonuses Just for You

8. Special Bonuses Just for You!

Chapter 8

Special Bonuses Just for You!

"I don't think bonuses are always bad."
~ Andrew Cuomo ~

You Made It this Far. You Deserve a Special Bonus

The average book sold is only read up to page eighteen. That's a very sad statistic.

How much information is being left on the table? How many people could be so much further along in their lives had they simply *read* the books available to them? Well, that's too bad for them.

Not you. You are not average. You are here to make a better life for yourself, your loved ones, and those who you will be solving problems for with your wholesaling skills.

I like to reward those who take action. And that is you! Because you have read this far and have diligently learned the few simple steps of wholesaling, I want to give you something.

First, I would like to share a little-known technique I use to find people who have properties they don't want, that are usually not listed for sale.

Go to the website for the county where you would like to find some properties. Look for the County Treasurer or the Department of Revenue. You want to find the office that handles unpaid real estate taxes.

Many county websites will have lists of people with unpaid taxes readily available, though some won't. You may have to call the ones that do not have the information posted online. Get a list of who is delinquent in their real estate tax.

Some counties are more user-friendly than others. They are usually happy to give you this information. You can go to any county in the country to search for properties this way.

This is a great way to *solve the county's problem.* They need their tax dollars to run the county.

When you get the list, contact the property owners on it. You can send them a letter or call them. The list will rarely include the owner's phone number but will almost always list the payors address.

Keep in mind that the property owner and the tax payor are not always the same person. Also, the owner and/or payor may have a different mailing address than the subject property.

Also, be aware that the property taxes are often not being paid because the owner has passed away or has moved. When you take a little time to hunt down the owner, you place yourself leaps and bounds ahead of your competition, most of whom choose to take the easiest path.

You can Google the payor and the property address and sometimes they will show up in your search results. There are some other websites that may have some more updated information than the county does. Some of these sites have information that you have to pay for.

A Couple of Bonus Nuggets for You – to Go Along with Your Bonus

Through all my years of investing, I have come across a few useful, but *FREE,* websites. The two I would like to share with you can save you an invaluable amount of time and money.

NETROnline.com

The first site I want to tell you about is one that will help you find county information. There are 3,142 counties and county equivalents in the United States. Each one is completely different, even those within the same state.

They all operate to the beat of their own drummer. Each one is independently owned and operated. If one doesn't work for you, start looking in another.

Keep in mind, that you can get a property under contract in a county far from your own and wholesale it to someone who lives in that area. You can be a *virtual bird dog* from the comfort of your own couch.

The site I use is NETROnline.com . This site has some paid services but it also has some very valuable free information.

When you visit the site, you will see some green tabs. One says *Public Records Online*. Clicking on it will open a map of the United States. Next click on the state that you want to look at.

This will open a page that lists the counties or equivalents for that state. Click on any county and it will bring up contact information to obtain the county's public records. Most counties have websites. Those that don't will only have phone numbers posted here.

Some counties have really good websites, and some have not-so-great sites. You can always call them to get the information you are looking for if navigating through their website is too cumbersome.

Many years ago, I paid more than $18,000 for a course I took just to find out about this site. I did get a lot more than just this at that training, of course. But this site alone has made me enough money by itself for a whole investment career.

I didn't share this information for many years. I'm happy to give it to you now since you are an action taker and I know it will serve you well. And yes, you are welcome.

TruePeopleSearch.com

Another Free site I would like to share with you is TruePeopleSearch.com . Simply enter the owner or tax payor's name, city and state or zip code. The site will show you the current known address and some other valuable information.

Sometimes it shows if the person has passed away. It shows previous and current addresses, phone numbers and sometimes email addresses and possible relatives.

This site gives you a lot of information at no cost. It does have some advertisers that have some pay-for-info services. I just use the free ones.

These sites are pretty accurate, but the information is not necessarily carved in stone. I would say they are about as accurate as my GPS I use when looking for a street address in the car. I give it about a 90% success rate. And that is actually pretty good for Free.

Another Priceless Bonus for You

The other thing I want to share with you, because you are an action taker, are my *Wholesaling Contracts*.

These are the two pieces of paper that I do all of my wholesaling with and I *gift* them to you. You can have the one-page contract that I use with my sellers* and the one-page assignment contract I use with my buyers.

One-Page Sales Contract with Seller

* If you prefer a multipage contract, you will need to seek those forms locally. You can ask at you REIA group, your attorney, or your state real estate commission.

CONTRACT TO PURCHASE REAL ESTATE

BE IT KNOWN The undersigned _____ and/or Assigns (Buyer), offers to purchase from _____
(Owner), real estate known as _____

City/Town of _____ County of _____ State of _____ said property more particularly described as

The purchase price offered is $ _____ **CASH**

Deposit herewith paid	$ _____
Balance at closing	$ _____
Total:	$ _____
	CASH

This contract is conditional upon the following terms:

1. This contract is for purchase of said property in "as is" condition.

2. This contract is subject to Buyer's approval and Buyer's partner's approval, in writing, of a walkthrough inspection of said property prior to closing.

3. Said property is to be sold free and clear of all encumbrances, by good and marketable title, with full possession to said property available to Buyer at date of closing.

4. The closing shall occur on or before _____ at the office of Buyer's escrow agent, unless such other time and place shall be agreed upon.

5. Other terms:

Signed this _____ day of _____, 20 20.

Buyer _____	Date _____
Buyer _____	Date _____
Seller _____	Date _____
Seller _____	Date _____

Assignment Contract with Buyer

Assignment of Contract

_____ Heartland Hideaways LLC _____ Assign's to _Branden Hurley & Tamara Gazillion_ the contract on (address) _3717 Lady, St Louis MO 63114_____

Between _____ Robert & Julia Maynard_ and _Heartland Hideaways LLC___
Dated _December 13, 2020_.

The contract is being assigned for the sum of _$5000___
Paid upon closing at closing.

Total sales Price including Contract & Assignments is $30000_ plus closing cost.

Assignee_____ Date _____

Buyer_____ Date _____

Buyer_____ Date _____

You can download these contracts directly from my website:

www.theDEALIONAIRE.com

Enter code: WINNER

Or, if you prefer, you can request them directly from me via email:

theDEALIONAIRE@gmail.com

Now You Are Ready to Follow These 3 Simple Steps Today!

9. Now You Are Ready to Follow These 3 Simple Steps Today!

Chapter 9

Now You Are Ready to Follow These 3 Simple Steps Today!

"But although all our knowledge begins with experience, it does not follow that it arises from experience."
~ Immanuel Kant ~

Ready. Set. Go!

You are now ready to implement the three simple steps that you've learned. You can immediately be on your way to making $5,000 to $10,000 in 30 days with No Cash, No Credit, and No problem!

Let's do a quick recap of the simple process you will start to follow today. Yes, **today**! All of the education in the world will not do you one bit of good unless you put it into action.

You've heard the saying *Knowledge is Power*. Well, *Knowledge without Action is Powerless*.

You can read all the books in the world. You can go to all the seminars and watch all the webinars presented by all the Gurus of the industry. Unless you do something with what you've learned, you might as well have been watching a rugby match.

So, I'm going to encourage you to get off your duff and actually do something. Put these simple steps into use. Sure, it takes a little bit of work, but the end result will make it worth your while.

I like Rhonda Byrne's book, *The Secret*. It's all about the "law of attraction." Whatever you focus on becomes real. It becomes you. It becomes part of your life and who you are.

I believe in positive thoughts and thinking the best of things. On the other hand, I believe that you cannot simply meditate with your bills and they will just go away. It doesn't work like that.

At least, it hasn't worked that way in the world I live in. And I'll guess it has not worked that way in your world either. It also does not take very much effort to become a *master wholesaler*.

Let's Review The 3 Simple Steps

Ok, so let's take a quick look and review what we've learned.

Step 1
What Are Screaming Deals for You?

When you first picked up this book, you may have had absolutely NO Cash, NO Credit and NO Clue what to do. Now you know what to do and where to start.

You probably had no idea what this Wholesaling thing was all about. Now you know that **Wholesaling** is a strategy where an average person can become an investor by simply putting a property under contract and then selling that contract, or paper, to another investor at a profit.

You didn't know what kinds of screaming deals to look for. Now you know that you are looking for properties that can be obtained at a significant discount. You are looking for homes that usually are in need of repair and cannot easily be sold retail.

Step 2
Where Do You Find Screaming Deals?

When you first picked up this book, you didn't know where to find these screaming deals. Now you know. You know that screaming deals are all around you.

They can be found online in ads. They can be found while you are driving or walking around. You can find them by talking to neighbors in the neighborhood.

You can post ads of your own. People that need to sell will call you after seeing your bandit signs. Screaming deals will come to you from word of mouth. Simply telling those you know what you are doing will usually generate leads and interest from sellers.

You can even create a team of Bird Dogs. Getting others to find you deals for a small fee can bring you a ton of screaming deals. You can also be a bird dog for other investors in your area when you are first starting out.

There are so many screaming deals all over the place and so many ways to find them. Be creative. Once you develop an eye for finding deals, they will seem to just come to you. Be the *screaming deal magnet*.

Step 3
What Do You Do with These Screaming Deals?

When you first started reading this book, you weren't sure what to do with a screaming deal once you got one. Now you know how easy it is to turn it into cash.

You know that there are only a couple of pieces of paper involved. You just need a sales contract from the seller to you and an assignment contract from you to your buyer.

There are only a couple of clauses you need to have in your contract in order to insure you do things the right way. You also know that you can walk away from a deal if it turns out that it's not really a deal at all.

You know to send your paperwork to a title company that is investor-friendly and knowledgeable. They will do the title search for you and make sure you have a good, transferable title.

You now know that finding end-buyers is actually one of the easiest parts of wholesaling. You now know you can find them at REIAs, by posting ads, through bandit signs, and by networking with those you know.

You now know how to make $5,000 to $10,000 in 30 days with NO Cash, NO Credit and NO Problem!

Now what? Where do you start? Let's make *your* plan.

Make YOUR Plan

Make a plan specific for you and follow it. Right now. Not Saturday. Not next week. Not tomorrow. Not even later today. Let's get started right **now**.

Get out a pen and paper or your smart phone or computer. I still prefer to use a paper notebook and pens. I use two pens, each with a different color ink, because it uses both sides of your brain — or so they say. I personally think it just makes it easier for me to find things later.

I also like carrying my notebook around with me for easy access. It comes in handy when I'm driving and see a prospective home, a bandit sign, or anything else I want to jot down and make note of.

Some of my friend's still joke about my *Dollar Store iPad,* as they like to call it. I don't care. It can get wet and I never have to worry about losing information because of a technical glitch.

Just use whatever works best for you. Whether you choose an old fashion notebook or an electronic device, just do it.

Start by putting together a list of potential screaming deals. Get your phone or computer out and look at some ads. Look on Craigslist and Zillow to start. There are many other places these deals can be found, even on auction sites like eBay!

Take your log with you wherever you go. These screaming deals are everywhere. Look for deals while driving, walking, and when talking and networking.

Find a deal and get it under contract *this week*. Send your paperwork to the title company. Find a cash buyer. Start working your next deal.

Don't just sit around waiting for your 30 days to pass.

Keep finding screaming deals. Don't stop with just one. Find one a week. Find one a day. Find two a day. The only thing limiting you is *you*.

Close your first deal in 30 days and **get paid!** Close two deals in 30 days and get paid. Close five deals in 30 days and get paid.

You will decide the amount of money you will make with these screaming deals. Go out and solve problems for others. We all have them.

Do something good for others today.

You'll Be Glad You Did!

Screaming Deals Are as Simple as 1, 2, 3

__1.__ What Are Screaming Deals for You?
__2.__ Where Do You Find Screaming Deals?
__3.__ What Do You Do with These Screaming Deals?

Lather. Rinse. Repeat.

Like my good friend **AJ Rassamni** says, *"Solve enough problems for enough people and you will get what you want."*

Tell me your success story. I want to hear your experience.

Contact me directly

theDealionaire@gmail.com

visit my website

theDealionaire.com

HAAs

Do You Know Your BOM from Their DOM?

"But why, why, why can't people just say what they mean?"
~ Graeme Simsion, The Rosie Project ~

Why Don't They Just Say What They Mean?

You'll see very quickly, that real estate people like to use hegemonies, abbreviations or acronyms instead of words. It used to drive me insane when I was a mortgage broker.

I like to call it, Real Estate **HAA.** *Hegemonies. Abbreviations & Acronyms.*

Hegemony simply means control or dominance by one group over others. Many in real estate like to think this is true.

It is not true.

Here are a few of the most commonly used **HAA**s to help ease your sanity.

APR	Annual Percentage Rate
ARM	Adjustable Rate Mortgage
ARV	After Repair Value
BOM	Bill of Materials
BPO	Broker's Price Opinion
BRRRR	Buy, Rehab, Rent, Refinance, Repeat
CAP	Capitalization Rate
COC	Cash On Cash (Return)
CMA	Comparative Market Analysis
DOM	Days on Market
DSCR	Debt Service Coverage Ratio
DTI	Debt to Income ration
EIN	Employer Identification Number
FDIC	Federal Deposit Insurance Corporation

FMV	Fair Market Value
FHA	Federal Housing Administration
FICO	Fair Isaac Corporation
GIP	Gross Investor Profit
HELOC	Home Equity Line of Credit
HOA	Home Owners Association
HUD	Housing and Urban Development
LRA	Land Reutilization Authority
LTV	Loan To Value
NOI	Net Operating income
MAO	Maximum Allowable Offer
MIP	Mortgage Insurance Premium
MLS	Multiple Listing Service
P&L	Profit and Loss Statement
PITI	Principal, Interest, Taxes & Insurance
PMI	Private Mortgage Insurance
POA	Property Owner Association
RCE	Repair Cost Estimate
REIA	Real Estate Investment Association
REO	Real Estate Owned-Bank Owned Properties
RESPA	Real Estate Settlement Procedures Act

ROI	Return on Investment
SDIRA	Self-Directed Individual Retirement Account
SFR	Single Family Residence
VA	Veterans Administration

Real Estate Investing Strategies

"Forecasts may tell you a great deal about the forecaster; they tell you nothing about the future." ~ Warren Buffett ~

Here's a Few Investing Strategies

BRRRR

Buy, Rehab, Rent, Refinance, Repeat. The goal behind a BRRRR strategy is to pull all of the money you put into a property out when you refinance it so that you effectively bought a property for nothing, but still have 25 percent built-in equity to reduce risk.

Buy and Hold / Rentals

Holding rental property for a period of time, during which the property pays for itself through rental income, producing cash to pay all expenses while also producing an annual profit for the owners. These properties can be sold for a profit as equity builds or held long-term to generate passive income. Most common are single family or 2-4 unit multifamily rental property. Others invest in mobile homes or self-storage units. Rental investors either manage properties themselves or hire a property manager.

Crowdfunding

Relatively new, investors are found online. The SEC allows only accredited investors to invest in individual assets that are crowdfunded.

Flipping

Buy a property, make improvements yourself or with contractors, and sell. Flippers take advantage of inefficiencies in the market, bringing a lot of experience to plan and oversee a project, then selling for (hopefully) a profit.

Notes

The origination of new, or the purchase of existing real estate secured mortgages and/or trust deeds. The terms of a mortgage are detailed in the promissory "note." The real estate is not owned by the note holder: the note holder has a lien position against the real estate. If the borrower breaches the terms of the loan agreement, the lien holder can foreclose upon their interest and acquire title to the property.

Private Lending or Partnering

Instead of being actively involved in house flipping or buying a rental property, you can be a private lender or equity partner. Let other people do all the work involved with finding deals, lining up projects, and filling apartments, but you get to earn some of the profits. All you have to do is vet the investor and underwrite the deals to make sure it makes sense.

Wholesaling

Wholesalers try to find and negotiate really good deals, then sell that contract to a house flipper or landlord. Wholesaling requires an investor to land a deal for cheap and sell that deal for a quick profit. Wholesale property prices are below retail price. If you want access to wholesale deals, you need to get on buyers lists.

Real Estate Math - Intentions

"Somehow it's o.k. for people to chuckle about not being good at math. Yet if I said 'I never learned to read,' they'd say I was an illiterate dolt."
~ Neil Degrasse Tyson ~

If All Goes Well... as Intended

ARV Calculation:
Price/Sq. Foot Avg. for the area X Subject Property sq. ft. = Anticipated ARV

Net operating income (NOI)
 NOI= annual income - operating expenses

(Operating Expenses: taxes, insurance, management, maintenance/repairs, utilities) NOT MORTGAGE

Return on Investment (ROI) ROI = NOI ÷ Cash Investment

Cash Flow = NOI - Mortgage

Cash on Cash Return (COC) – (for the 1st year of the investment)
COC = Cash Flow ÷ Cash In (down payment and closing costs)

Capitalization Rate (Cap Rate) %
Cap Rate = NOI ÷ Purchase Price

Debt Service Coverage Ratio (DSCR)
DCSR = (NOI) ÷ annual mortgage debt (principal + interest)

Maximum Allowable Offer (MAO)
ARV (after repair value)
X .7 or .65 (This multiplier changes based on your market)
- Repairs
- Profit
=Max Offer

Real Estate Jargon

"There's nothing quite like Latin for disguising the fact that you're making it up as you go along."
~ Ben Aaronovitch, British Author ~

Acceleration Clause
A clause in your mortgage, which allows the lender to demand payment of the outstanding loan balance for various reasons. The most common reasons for accelerating a loan are if the borrower defaults on the loan or transfers title to another individual without informing the lender.

Adjustable Rate Mortgage (ARM)
A mortgage in which the interest changes periodically, according to corresponding fluctuations in an index. All ARMs are tied to indexes.

Adjustment Date
The date the interest rate changes on an adjustable-rate mortgage (ARM).

Amortization
The loan payment consists of a portion which will be applied to pay the accruing interest on a loan, with the remainder being applied to the principal. Over time, the interest portion decreases as the loan balance decreases, and the amount applied to principal increases so that the loan is paid off (amortized) in the specified time.

Amortization Schedule
A table which shows how much of each payment will be applied toward principal and how much toward interest over the life of the loan. It also shows the gradual decrease of the loan balance until it reaches zero.

Annual Percentage Rate (APR)
This is not the note rate on your loan. It is a value created according to a government formula intended to reflect the true annual cost of borrowing, expressed as a percentage. It works sort of like this, but not exactly, so only use this as a guideline: deduct the closing costs from your loan amount, then using your actual loan payment, calculate what the interest rate would be on this amount instead of your actual loan amount. You will come up with a number close to the APR. Because you are using the same payment

on a smaller amount, the APR is always higher than the actual not rate on your loan.

Application
The form used to apply for a mortgage loan, containing information about a borrower's income, savings, assets, debts, and more.

Appraisal
A written justification of the price paid for a property, primarily based on an analysis of comparable sales of similar homes nearby.

Appraised Value
An opinion of a property's fair market value, based on an appraiser's knowledge, experience, and analysis of the property. Since an appraisal is based primarily on comparable sales, and the most recent sale is the one on the property in question, the appraisal usually comes out at the purchase price.

Appraiser
An individual qualified by education, training, and experience to estimate the value of real property and personal property. Although some appraisers work directly for mortgage lenders, most are independent.

Appreciation
The increase in the value of a property due to changes in market conditions, inflation, or other causes.

Assessed value
The valuation placed on property by a public tax assessor for purposes of taxation.

Assessment
The placing of a value on property for the purpose of taxation.

Assessor
A public official who establishes the value of a property for taxation purposes.

Asset
Items of value owned by an individual. Assets that can be quickly converted into cash are considered "liquid assets." These include bank accounts, stocks, bonds, mutual funds, and so on. Other assets include real estate, personal property, and debts owed to an individual by others.

Assignment
When ownership of your mortgage is transferred from one company or individual to another, it is called an assignment.

Assignment Fee
Encompasses the transfer of rights held by one party, the assignor, to another party, the assignee. An assignment allows another buyer to take over the buyer's rights. Imagine that one is stepping into the shoes of the Original Purchaser for a **fee** in order to purchase the desired property.

Assumable mortgage
A mortgage that can be assumed by the buyer when a home is sold. Usually, the borrower must "qualify" in order to assume the loan.

Assumption
The term applied when a buyer assumes the seller's mortgage.

Balloon mortgage
A mortgage loan that requires the remaining principal balance be paid at a specific point in time. For example, a loan may be amortized as if it would be paid over a thirty year period, but requires that at the end of the tenth year the entire remaining balance must be paid.

Balloon payment
The final lump sum payment that is due at the termination of a balloon mortgage.

Bankruptcy
By filing in federal bankruptcy court, an individual or individuals can restructure or relieve themselves of debts and liabilities. Bankruptcies are of various types, but the most common for an individual seem to be a "Chapter 7 No Asset" bankruptcy which relieves the borrower of most types of debts. A borrower cannot usually qualify for an "A" paper loan for a period of two years after the bankruptcy has been discharged and requires the re-establishment of an ability to repay debt.

Bill of Sale
A written document that transfers title to personal property. For example, when selling an automobile to acquire funds which will be used as a source of down payment or for closing costs, the lender will usually require the bill of sale (in addition to other items) to help document this source of funds.

Biweekly Mortgage
A mortgage in which you make payments every two weeks instead of once a month. The basic result is that instead of making twelve monthly payments during the year, you make thirteen. The extra payment reduces the principal, substantially reducing the time it takes to pay off a thirty-year mortgage. *Note:* there are independent companies that encourage you to set up bi-weekly payment schedules with them on your thirty-year mortgage. They charge a set-up fee and a transfer fee for every payment. Your funds are deposited into a trust account from which your monthly payment is then made, and the excess funds then remain in the trust account until enough has accrued to make the additional payment which will then be paid to reduce your principle. You could save money by doing the same thing yourself, plus you have to have faith that once you transfer money to them that they will actually transfer your funds to your lender.

Blanket mortgage
A mortgage covering more than one piece of property. Example: A developer subdivides a tract of land into lots and obtains a blanket mortgage on the whole tract.

Bond
A promise by a third party to repay a principal and interest if another party does not make payment.

Bond Market
Usually refers to the daily buying and selling of thirty-year treasury bonds. Lenders follow this market intensely because as the yields of bonds go up and down, fixed rate mortgages do approximately the same thing. The same factors that affect the Treasury Bond market also affect mortgage rates at the same time. That is why rates change daily, and in a volatile market can and do change during the day as well.

Bridge Loan
Not used much anymore, bridge loans are obtained by those who have not yet sold their previous property but must close on a purchase property. The bridge loan becomes the source of their funds for the down payment. One reason for their fall from favor is that there are more and more second mortgage lenders now that will lend at a high loan to value. In addition, sellers often prefer to accept offers from buyers who have already sold their property.

Broker

Broker has several meanings in different situations. Most Realtors are "agents" who work under a "broker." Some agents are brokers as well, either working form themselves or under another broker. In the mortgage industry, broker usually refers to a company or individual that does not lend the money for the loans themselves, but broker loans to larger lenders or investors. (See the Home Loan Library that discusses the different types of lenders). As a normal definition, a broker is anyone who acts as an agent, bringing two parties together for any type of transaction and earns a fee for doing so.

Broker's Price Opinion

A BPO is the process used by a hired sales agent to determine the potential selling price or estimated **value** of a real estate property. A BPO is popularly used in situations where a financial institution believes the expense and delay of an appraisal is unnecessary.

Buydown

Usually refers to a fixed rate mortgage where the interest rate is "bought down" for a temporary period, usually one to three years. After that time and for the remainder of the term, the borrower's payment is calculated at the note rate. In order to buy down the initial rate for the temporary payment, a lump sum is paid and held in an account used to supplement the borrower's monthly payment. These funds usually come from the seller (or some other source) as a financial incentive to induce someone to buy their property. A "lender funded buydown" is when the lender pays the initial lump sum. They can accomplish this because the note rate on the loan (after the buydown adjustments) will be higher than the current market rate. One reason for doing this is because the borrower may get to "qualify" at the start rate and can qualify for a higher loan amount. Another reason is that a borrower may expect his earnings to go up substantially in the near future but wants a lower payment right now.

Call Option
Similar to the acceleration clause.

Cap
Adjustable Rate Mortgages have fluctuating interest rates, but those fluctuations are usually limited to a certain amount. Those limitations may apply to how much the loan may adjust over a six-month period, an annual period, and over the life of the loan, and are referred to as "caps." Some ARMs, although they may have a life cap, allow the interest rate to fluctuate freely, but require a certain minimum payment which can change once a year. There is a limit on how much that payment can change each year, and that limit is also referred to as a cap.

Capital gains
Profit earned from the sale of real estate or the amount by which an asset's selling price exceeds its initial purchase price.

Capitalization rate (CAP Rate)
The rate used to determine the present value of property with future earnings.

Carrying Costs
The expenses of maintaining a home or property. For example, mortgage payments, property taxes, insurance, and the expenses of utilities, repairs and upkeep.

Cash Flow
The amount of cash derived over a certain period of time from an income-producing property. Cash receipts minus cash payments over a given period of time. The cash flow should be large enough to pay the expenses of the income-producing property (mortgage payment, maintenance, utilities, etc.).

Cash Out Refinance
When a borrower refinances his mortgage at a higher amount than the current loan balance with the intention of pulling out money for personal use, it is referred to as a "cash out refinance."

Caveat Emptor
A legal term meaning "let buyer beware". The buyer must examine the property and buy at his/her own risk. Example: A property may be offered in an "as is" condition with no expressed or implied guarantee of quality or condition.

Certificate of Deposit
A time deposit held in a bank which pays a certain amount of interest to the depositor.

Certificate of Deposit Index
One of the indexes used for determining interest rate changes on some adjustable rate mortgages. It is an average of what banks are paying on certificates of deposit.

Certificate of Eligibility
A document issued by the Veterans Administration that certifies a veteran's eligibility for a VA loan.

Certificate of occupancy
Document issued by a local governmental agency that states a property meets the local building standards for occupancy and is in compliance with public health and building codes. This document is normally required by a lender prior to closing the loan.

Certificate of Reasonable Value (CRV)
Once the appraisal has been performed on a property being bought with a VA loan, the Veterans Administration issues a CRV.

Chain of Title
An analysis of the transfers of title to a piece of property over the years.

Clear Title
A title that is free of liens or legal questions as to ownership of the property.

Closing
This has different meanings in different states. In some states a real estate transaction is not consider "closed" until the documents record at the local recorder's office. In others, the "closing" is a meeting where all of the documents are signed and money changes hands.

Closing Costs
Closing costs are separated into what are called "non-recurring closing costs" and "pre-paid items." Non-recurring closing costs are any items which are paid just once as a result of buying the property or obtaining a loan. "Pre-paids" are items which recur over time, such as property taxes and homeowner's insurance. A lender makes an attempt to estimate the amount of non-recurring closing costs and prepaid items on the Good Faith Estimate which they must issue to the borrower

within three days of receiving a home loan application.

Closing Statement
See Settlement Statement.

Cloud on Title
Any conditions revealed by a title search that adversely affect the title to real estate. Usually clouds on title cannot be removed except by deed, release, or court action.

Co-Borrower
An additional individual who is both obligated on the loan and is on title to the property.

Collateral
In a home loan, the property is the collateral. The borrower risks losing the property if the loan is not repaid according to the terms of the mortgage or deed of trust.

Collection
When a borrower falls behind, the lender contacts them in an effort to bring the loan current. The loan goes to "collection." As part of the collection effort, the lender must mail and record certain documents in case they are eventually required to foreclose on the property.

Commission
Most salespeople earn commissions for the work that they do and there are many sales professionals involved in each transaction, including Realtors, loan officers, title representatives, attorneys, escrow representative, and representatives for pest companies, home warranty companies, home inspection companies, insurance agents, and more. The commissions are paid out of the charges paid by the seller or buyer in the purchase transaction. Realtors generally earn the largest commissions, followed by lenders, then the others.

Common Area Assessments
In some areas they are called Homeowners Association Fees. They are charges paid to the Homeowners Association by the owners of the individual units in a condominium or planned unit development (PUD) and are generally used to maintain the property and common areas.

Common Areas
Those portions of a building, land, and amenities owned (or managed) by a planned unit development (PUD) or condominium project's homeowners' association (or a cooperative project's cooperative corporation) that are used by all of the unit owners, who share in the common expenses of their operation and maintenance. Common areas include swimming pools, tennis courts, and other recreational facilities, as well as

common corridors of buildings, parking areas, means of ingress and egress, etc.

Common Law
An unwritten body of law based on general custom in England and used to an extent in some states.

Community Property
In some states, especially the southwest, property acquired by a married couple during their marriage is considered to be owned jointly, except under special circumstances. This is an outgrowth of the Spanish and Mexican heritage of the area.

Comparative Market Analysis (CMA)
A comparison of sales prices of similar properties in a given area for the purpose of determining the fair market value of a property. Also referred to as "Comps."

Comparable Sales
Recent sales of similar properties in nearby areas and used to help determine the market value of a property. Also referred to as "comps."

Conditional Commitment
A written document provided by a lender agreeing to make a loan provided certain conditions are met by the borrower prior to closing.

Condominium
A type of ownership in real property where all of the owners own the property, common areas and buildings together, with the exception of the interior of the unit to which they have title. Often mistakenly referred to as a type of construction or development, it actually refers to the type of ownership.

Condominium Conversion
Changing the ownership of an existing building (usually a rental project) to the condominium form of ownership.

Condominium Hotel
A condominium project that has rental or registration desks, short-term occupancy, food and telephone services, and daily cleaning services and that is operated as a commercial hotel even though the units are individually owned. These are often found in resort areas like Hawaii.

Consideration
Anything of value given to induce another to enter into a contract. An earnest money deposit on a sales contract is consideration.

Construction Loan
A short-term, interim loan for financing the cost of construction. The lender makes payments to the builder at periodic intervals as the work progresses.

Contingency
A condition that must be met before a contract is legally binding. For example, home purchasers often include a contingency that specifies that the contract is not binding until the purchaser obtains a satisfactory home inspection report from a qualified home inspector.

Contract
An oral or written agreement to do or not to do a certain thing.

Contract for Deed
A real estate installment selling arrangement where the buyer may occupy the property, but the seller retains the title until the agreed upon sales price has been paid. Also known as an installment land contract.

Conventional Mortgage
Refers to home loans other than government loans (VA and FHA).

Convertible ARM
An adjustable-rate mortgage that allows the borrower to change the ARM to a fixed-rate mortgage within a specific time.

Conveyance
The transfer of title of real property from one party to another.

Cooperative (co-op)
A type of multiple ownership in which the residents of a multiunit housing complex own shares in the cooperative corporation that owns the property, giving each resident the right to occupy a specific apartment or unit.

Cost of Funds Index (COFI)
One of the indexes that is used to determine interest rate changes for certain adjustable-rate mortgages. It represents the weighted-average cost of savings, borrowings, and advances of the financial institutions such as banks and savings & loans, in the 11th District of the Federal Home Loan Bank.

Credit
An agreement in which a borrower receives something of value in exchange for a promise to repay the lender at a later date.

Credit History
A record of an individual's repayment of debt. Credit histories are reviewed my mortgage lenders as one of the underwriting criteria in determining credit risk.

Creditor
A person to whom money is owed.Credit Report
A report of an individual's credit history prepared by a credit bureau and used by a lender in determining a loan applicant's credit worthiness.

Credit Repository
An organization that gathers, records, updates, and stores financial and public records information about the payment records of individuals who are being considered for credit.

Debt
An amount owed to another.

Debt Service Coverage Ratio (DSCR)
A benchmark used by lenders when measuring an income property's ability to cover the mortgage debt after operating expenses is the Debt Service Coverage Ratio (DCSR). The DCSR is calculated by dividing the Net Operating Income (NOI) by the annual mortgage debt (principal + interest).

Debt-to-Income Ratio
The ratio, expressed as a percentage, which results when a borrower's monthly payment obligation on long-term debts is divided by his or her net effective income (FHA/ VA loans) or gross monthly income (conventional loans).

Deed
The legal document conveying title to a property.

Deed In Lieu
Short for "deed in lieu of foreclosure," this conveys title to the lender when the borrower is in default and wants to avoid foreclosure. The lender may or may not cease foreclosure activities if a borrower asks to provide a deed-in-lieu. Regardless of

whether the lender accepts the deed-in-lieu, the avoidance and non-repayment of debt will most likely show on a credit history. What a deed-in-lieu may prevent is having the documents preparatory to a foreclosure being recorded and become a matter of public record.

Deed of Trust
Some states, like California, do not record mortgages. Instead, they record a deed of trust which is essentially the same thing.

Default
Failure to make the mortgage payment within a specified period of time. For first mortgages or first trust deeds, if a payment has still not been made within 30 days of the due date, the loan is considered to be in default.

Defective Title
Any recorded instrument that would prevent a grantor/seller from giving a clear title.

Delinquency
Failure to make mortgage payments when mortgage payments are due. For most mortgages, payments are due on the first day of the month. Even though they may not charge a "late fee" for a number of days, the payment is still considered to be late and the loan delinquent. When a loan payment is more than 30 days late, most lenders report the late payment to one or more credit bureaus.

Deposit
A sum of money given in advance of a larger amount being expected in the future. Often called in real estate as an "earnest money deposit."

Depreciation
A decline in the value of property; the opposite of appreciation. Depreciation is also an accounting term which shows the declining monetary value of an asset and is used as an expense to reduce taxable income. Since this is not a true expense where money is actually paid, lenders will add back depreciation expense for self-employed borrowers and count it as income.

Disbursement
(a) The payment of loan money to the borrower usually at or following the closing; (b) Funds paid.

Discount Points
In the mortgage industry, this term is usually used in only in reference to government loans, meaning FHA and VA loans. Discount points refer to any "points" paid in addition to the one percent loan origination fee. A "point" is one percent of the loan amount.

Down Payment
The part of the purchase price of a property that the buyer pays in cash and does not finance with a mortgage.

Due On Sale Provision/Clause
A provision in a mortgage that allows the lender to demand repayment in full if the borrower sells the property that serves as security for the mortgage.

Earnest Money Deposit
A deposit made by the potential home buyer to show that he or she is serious about buying the house.

Easement
A right of way giving persons other than the owner access to or over a property.

Effective Age
An appraiser's estimate of the physical condition of a building. The actual age of a building may be shorter or longer than its effective age.

Eminent Domain
The right of a government to take private property for public use upon payment of its fair market value. Eminent domain is the basis for condemnation proceedings.

Employer Identification Number (EIN)
Also known as a Federal Tax Identification Number is used to identify a business entity. A new business must file for an identification number with the IRS. An EIN is your permanent number and can be used immediately to open a

bank account, for business licenses, and file a tax return by mail.

Encroachment
An improvement that intrudes illegally on another's property.

Encumbrance
Anything that affects or limits the fee simple title to a property, such as mortgages, leases, easements, or restrictions.

Equal Credit Opportunity Act (ECOA)
A federal law that requires lenders and other creditors to make credit equally available without discrimination based on race, color, religion, national origin, age, sex, marital status, or receipt of income from public assistance programs.

Equity
A homeowner's financial interest in a property. Equity is the difference between the fair market value of the property and the amount still owed on its mortgage and other liens.

Equity Partnership
A limited partnership that provides start-up capital to businesses.

Escheat
The reversion of property to the state in the event that the owner dies without leaving a will and has no legal heirs.

Escrow
An item of value, money, or documents deposited with a third party to be delivered upon the fulfillment of a condition. For example, the earnest money deposit is put into escrow until delivered to the seller when the transaction is closed.

Escrow Account
Once you close your purchase transaction, you may have an escrow account or impound account with your lender. This means the amount you pay each month includes an amount above what would be required if you were only paying your principal and interest. The extra money is held in your impound account (escrow account) for the payment of items like property taxes and homeowner's insurance when they come due. The lender pays them with your money instead of you paying them yourself.

Escrow Analysis
Once each year your lender will perform an "escrow analysis" to make sure they are collecting the correct amount of money for the anticipated expenditures.

Escrow Disbursements
The use of escrow funds to pay real estate taxes, hazard insurance, mortgage insurance, and other property expenses as they become due.

Estate
The ownership interest of an individual in real property. The sum total of all the real property and personal property owned by an individual at time of death.

Eviction
The lawful expulsion of an occupant from real property.

Examination of Title
The report on the title of a property from the public records or an abstract of the title.

Exclusive Listing
A written contract that gives a licensed real estate agent the exclusive right to sell a property for a specified time.

Executor
A person named in a will to administer an estate. The court will appoint an administrator if no executor is named. "Executrix" is the feminine form.

Exit Strategy
Money is often made with investment real estate when it is sold. And even if the property is held in order to build equity, a great deal of the profit is made when exiting the investment. Therefore, an exit strategy is essential to making money with real estate.

5 top exit strategies for real estate investors to consider:
Wholesale, Flip, Buy and Hold to Build Equity, Seller Financing, Lease Option or Rent-to-Own.

Fair Credit Reporting Act
A consumer protection law that regulates the disclosure of consumer credit reports by consumer/credit reporting agencies and establishes procedures for correcting mistakes on one's credit record.

Fannie Mae/Federal National mortgage Association (FNMA)
A federal organization that purchases loans from lenders and then sells them as FNMA mortgage backed securities.

Farmers Home Administration (FMHA)
An agency, within the U.S. Department of Agriculture, that makes and insures loans for rural housing and farms.

Federal Deposit Insurance Corporation (FDIC)
A government agency that supervises and insures accounts held by lending institutions.

Fee Simple (Fee Absolute or Fee Simple Absolute) Absolute ownership of real property; owner is entitled to the entire property with unrestricted power of disposition during the owner's life and upon his death the property descends to the owner's designated heirs.

Federal Housing Administration (FHA)
A government agency within HUD that administers and insures mortgage loans for private lending agencies.

FHA Loan
This program provides mortgage insurance to protect lenders against the risk of default on loans to qualified buyers. A loan insured by the Federal Housing Administration is open to all qualified home purchasers.

FICO (Fair Isaac Corporation)
The first company to offer a credit-risk model with a **score**. Credit scores are reported by three major credit bureaus, Equifax, Experian and Trans-Union. Scores are not necessarily the same on each bureau's report because each bureau may place a slightly different value on different items.
Model Factors: payment history, outstanding debt, length of history, inquiries, types of credit in use.
By law, everyone is entitled to receive one free credit report from each of the three major credit bureaus every 12 months.

Fair Market Value (FMV)
The highest price that a buyer, willing but not compelled to buy, would pay, and the lowest a

seller, willing but not compelled to sell, would accept.

Fannie Mae (FNMA)
The Federal National Mortgage Association, which is a congressionally chartered, shareholder-owned company that is the nation's largest supplier of home mortgage funds. For a discussion of the roles of Fannie Mae, Freddie Mac (FHLMC), and Ginnie Mae (GNMA), see the Library.

Fannie Mae's Community Home Buyer's Program
An income-based community lending model, under which mortgage insurers and Fannie Mae offer flexible underwriting guidelines to increase a low- or moderate-income family's buying power and to decrease the total amount of cash needed to purchase a home. Borrowers who participate in this model are required to attend pre-purchase home-buyer education sessions.

Federal Housing Administration (FHA)
An agency of the U.S. Department of Housing and Urban Development (HUD). Its main activity is the insuring of residential mortgage loans made by private lenders. The FHA sets standards for construction and underwriting but does not lend money or plan or construct housing.

Fee Simple
The greatest possible interest a person can have in real estate.

Fee Simple Estate
An unconditional, unlimited estate of inheritance that represents the greatest estate and most extensive interest in land that can be enjoyed. It is of perpetual duration. When the real estate is in a condominium project, the unit owner is the exclusive owner only of the air space within his or her portion of the building (the unit) and is an owner in common with respect to the land and other common portions of the property.

FHA Mortgage
A mortgage that is insured by the Federal Housing Administration (FHA). Along with VA loans, an FHA loan will often be referred to as a government loan.

Fiduciary
A company that holds the assets of another party and invests them on behalf of the party.

Finance Charge
Interest charged by a lender.

Financial Reports
Reports such as income statements, cash flows, and balance sheets that are used when documenting the financial aspects of your business.

Firm Commitment
A lender's agreement to make a loan to a specific borrower on a specific property.

First Mortgage
The mortgage that is in first place among any loans recorded against a property. Usually refers to the date in which loans are recorded, but there are exceptions.

Fiscal Year
An accounting period consisting of 12 months.

Fixed Cost
A cost that does not vary with the volume of sales or production.

Fixed Rate Mortgage
A mortgage in which the interest rate does not change during the entire term of the loan.

Fixture
Personal property that becomes real property when attached in a permanent manner to real estate.

Flood Insurance
Insurance that compensates for physical property damage resulting from flooding. It is required for properties located in federally designated flood areas.

Forbearance
A lenders postponement of foreclosure in order to give the borrower time and an opportunity to make up for overdue payments. Also, an

agreement for a buyer to temporarily make higher payments in order to satisfy overdue payments.

Foreclosure
The legal process by which a borrower in default under a mortgage is deprived of his or her interest in the mortgaged property. This usually involves a forced sale of the property at public auction with the proceeds of the sale being applied to the mortgage debt.

Free and Clear
A property that has no liens.

FSBO (For Sale By Owner)
A property for sale that is not listed with a real estate broker and therefore will not be listed on the Multiple Listing Service (MLS).

401(k)/403(b)
An employer-sponsored investment plan that allows individuals to set aside tax-deferred income for retirement or emergency purposes. 401(k) plans are provided by employers that are private corporations. 403(b) plans are provided by employers that are not for profit organizations.

401(k)/403(b) loan
Some administrators of 401(k)/403(b) plans allow for loans against the monies you have accumulated in these plans. Loans against 401K plans are an acceptable source of down payment for most types of loans.

Government Loan (Mortgage)
A mortgage that is insured by the Federal Housing Administration (FHA) or guaranteed by the Department of Veterans Affairs (VA) or the Rural Housing Service (RHS). Mortgages that are not government loans are classified as conventional loans.

Government National Mortgage Association (Ginnie Mae)
A government-owned corporation within the U.S. Department of Housing and Urban Development (HUD). Created by Congress on September 1, 1968, GNMA performs the same role as Fannie Mae and Freddie Mac in providing funds to lenders for making home loans. The difference is that Ginnie Mae provides funds for government loans (FHA and VA)

Grace Period
The period from the time a payment is due to the point at which a creditor will take legal action.

Grantee
The person to whom an interest in real property is conveyed.

Grantor
The person conveying an interest in real property.

Hard Money Lender - Lenders who use private money to make loans with Borrowers who have trouble getting loans via conventional methods. There is usually a very high interest rate associated with hard money lenders.

Hazard Insurance
Insurance coverage that in the event of physical damage to a property from fire, wind, vandalism, or other hazards.

Home Equity Conversion Mortgage (HECM)
Usually referred to as a reverse annuity mortgage, what makes this type of mortgage unique is that instead of making payments to a lender, the lender makes payments to you. It enables older home owners to convert the equity they have in their homes into cash, usually in the form of monthly payments. Unlike traditional home equity loans, a borrower does not qualify on the basis of income but on the value of his or her home. In addition, the loan does not have to be repaid until the borrower no longer occupies the property.

Home Equity line of Credit (HELOC)
A mortgage loan, usually in second position, that allows the borrower to obtain cash drawn against the equity of his home, up to a predetermined amount.

Home Inspection
A thorough inspection by a professional that evaluates the structural and mechanical condition of a property. A satisfactory home inspection is often included as a contingency by the purchaser.

Homeowners' Association (HOA)
A nonprofit association that manages the common areas of a planned unit development (PUD) or condominium project. In a condominium project, it has no ownership interest in the common elements. In a PUD project, it holds title to the common elements.

Homeowner's Insurance
An insurance policy that combines personal liability insurance and hazard insurance coverage for a dwelling and its contents.

Homeowner's Warranty
A type of insurance often purchased by homebuyers that will cover repairs to certain items, such as heating or air conditioning, should they break down within the coverage period. The buyer often requests the seller to pay for this coverage as a condition of the sale, but either party can pay.

Homestead
Status provided to a homeowner's principal residence in some states that protects the home against certain judgments up to specified amounts.

Homestead exemption
Available in some states - this causes the assessed value of a principal residence to be reduced by the amount of the exemption for the purposes of calculating property tax.

Housing and Urban Development (HUD)
A U.S. government agency established to implement certain federal housing and community development programs.

Housing Choice Voucher
Formerly known as Section Eight, is a rental assistance program funded by the U.S. Department of Housing and Urban Development (HUD). The program allows low-income families, elderly and disabled households to find affordable housing in the private market and receive assistance in paying their monthly rent. Qualified participants receive a voucher and may choose from a variety of housing options, including apartments, duplexes, single-family homes and townhomes where the owner agrees to rent under the program. Rental units must meet minimum standards of health and safety, as determined by HASLC. A housing subsidy is paid to the landlord directly by HASLC on behalf of the participating family. The family then pays the difference between the actual rent charged by the landlord under the Housing Assistance Payment (HAP) contract and the amount subsidized by the program.

HUD Median Income
Median family income for a particular county or metropolitan statistical area (MSA), as estimated by the Department of Housing and Urban Development (HUD).

HUD-1 Settlement Statement
A document that provides an itemized listing of the funds that were paid at closing. Items that appear on the statement include real estate commissions, loan fees, points, and initial escrow (impound) amounts. Each type of expense goes on a specific numbered line on the sheet. The totals at the bottom of the HUD-1 statement define the seller's net proceeds and the buyer's net payment at closing. It is called a HUD1 because the form is printed by the Department of Housing and Urban Development (HUD). The HUD1 statement is also known as the "closing statement" or "settlement sheet."

Improvements
Additions to raw land such as buildings, streets, etc. that add value to the land.

Income Approach
A method used by an appraiser to estimate the value of rental property based on the income it generates over the life of the structure, discounted to determine its present value.

Income Property
Real estate that generates revenue such as rental income.

Ingress and Egress
The right to go in and out over a piece of property but not the right to park on it. See also Easements.

Inspection
An examination of a property or building to determine condition or quality for a particular purpose such as an assessment of structural or termite damage. An inspection may also be used to con rm that the property meets the standards of the contract.

Installment sale
See land contract.

Interest Cap
A limit on the amount that the interest rate for an adjustable rate mortgage can change, regardless of how much the index changes. Most ARMs have a cap on both the amount they can increase and decrease at any periodic adjustment interval, and a life-long cap that limits the amount the interest rate can vary over the life of the loan. The two interest caps are sometimes called a "periodic cap" and a "life cap".

Interest rate
The percentage rate on a principal amount charged by a lender for the use of a sum of money.

Investor
A money source for a lender. Also, one who makes investments.

Joint Tenancy
A form of ownership or taking title to property which means each party owns the whole property and that ownership is not separate. In the event of the death of one party, the survivor owns the property in its entirety.

Joint venture
An agreement between two or more parties that out- lines the financial terms of their interaction, the role and duties of each party, and the intended outcome of the project they will be collectively working on.

Judgment
A decision made by a court of law. In judgments that require the repayment of a debt, the court may place a lien against the debtor's real property as collateral for the judgment's creditor. Alternative spelling is "judgment."

Judicial Foreclosure
A type of foreclosure proceeding used in some states that is handled as a civil lawsuit and conducted entirely under the auspices of a court. Other states use non-judicial foreclosure.

Jumbo Loan
A loan that exceeds Fannie Mae's and Freddie Mac's loan limits, currently at $227,150. Also called a nonconforming loan. Freddie Mac and Fannie Mae loans are referred to as conforming loans.

Junior Lien
A lien which is in a subordinate position to other liens existing on a property.

Junior mortgage
All mortgages/liens subordinate to the rst mortgage.

Land Contract
A real estate installment selling arrangement where-by the buyer may use and occupy land, but ownership of the property is not transferred until all the payments have been made.

Landlord
The owner of real property who rents or leases to another party, called a tenant.

Land trust
A revocable trust agreement usually used in conjunction with a piece of property. The managing party of the agreement, the Trustee, is named in public records while the Beneficiary is not disclosed.

Lease
A written agreement between the property owner and a tenant that stipulates the payment and conditions under which the tenant may possess the real estate for a specified period of time.

Lease Option
An alternative financing option that allows home buyers to lease a home with an option to buy. Each month's rent payment may consist of not only the rent, but an additional amount which can be applied toward the down payment on an already specified price.

Leasehold Estate
A way of holding title to a property wherein the mortgagor does not actually own the property but rather has a recorded long-term lease on it.

Legal Description
A property description, recognized by law, that is sufficient to locate and identify the property without oral testimony.

Legal Rate of Interest
The legal amount a lender can charge a borrower on a loan. This varies from state to state.

Lender
A term which can refer to the institution making the loan or to the individual representing the firm. For example, loan officers are often referred to as "lenders."

Lender seasoning
An ownership time requirement from many lenders that can limit the ability to buy and immediately sell property. The extent to which this

is enforced may vary considerably from state to state.

Lessee
A person who leases a property from its owner.
(Tenant)

Lessor
A person who rents property to another under a lease.
(Landlord)

Liabilities
A person's financial obligations. Liabilities include long-term and short-term debt, as well as any other amounts that are owed to others.

Liability Insurance
Insurance coverage that offers protection against claims alleging that a property owner's negligence or inappropriate action resulted in bodily injury or property damage to another party. It is usually part of a homeowner's insurance policy.

Lien
A legal claim against a property that must be paid off when the property is sold. A mortgage or first trust deed is considered a lien.

Lien Waiver
A document from a contractor, subcontractor, materials supplier, equipment lessor or other party to the construction project (the claimant) stating

they have received payment and waive any future lien rights to the property (of the owner) for the amount paid.

Life Cap
For an adjustable-rate mortgage (ARM), a limit on the amount that the interest rate can increase or decrease over the life of the mortgage.

Limited Power of Attorney
A document giving an investor the ability to control certain or all facets of the sale of a property on behalf of the owner, including the ability to sign on their behalf.

Lis Pendens
Latin term for "Lawsuit Pending"

Line of Credit
An agreement by a commercial bank or other financial institution to extend credit up to a certain amount for a certain time to a specified borrower.

Liquid Asset
A cash asset or an asset that is easily converted into cash.

Loan
A sum of borrowed money (principal) that is generally repaid with interest.

Loan Agreement
The arrangement of payments, conditions, and restrictions signed by the borrower of a loan.

Loan application
A document required by a lender prior to loan approval. The application includes detailed information about the borrower, their finances, and the property.

Loan Officer (LO)
Also referred to by a variety of other terms, such as lender, loan representative, loan "rep," account executive, and others. The loan officer serves several functions and has various responsibilities: they solicit loans, they are the representative of the lending institution, and they represent the borrower to the lending institution.

Loan Origination
How a lender refers to the process of obtaining new loans.

Loan Servicing
After you obtain a loan, the company you make the payments to is "servicing" your loan. They process payments, send statements, manage the escrow/impound account, provide collection efforts on delinquent loans, ensure that insurance and property taxes are made on the property, handle pay-offs and assumptions, and provide a variety of other services

Loan To Value (LTV)
The percentage relationship between the amount of the loan and the appraised value or sales price (whichever is lower).

Lock In
An agreement in which the lender guarantees a specified interest rate for a certain amount of time at a certain cost.

Lock In Period
The time period during which the lender has guaranteed an interest rate to a borrower.

Manufactured Home
Homes built in a factory-controlled environment and that meet strict HUD codes. They are brought to the property site and are assembled there.

Margin
The difference between the interest rate and the index on an adjustable rate mortgage. The margin remains stable over the life of the loan. It is the index which moves up and down.

Maris

Mid America Regional Information Systems (MARIS) administers the Multiple Listing Service (MLS) for the St. Louis, St. Charles County, Jefferson and County Associations and the Franklin County, East Central, South Central and Pulaski County Boards of REALTORS®. The MLS website contains information to help agents achieve the goal of listing and selling real estate.

Market value
The highest price that a buyer would pay and the lowest price a seller would accept on a property.

Maturity
The date on which the principal balance of a loan, bond, or other financial instrument becomes due and payable.

Merged Credit Report
A credit report which reports the raw data pulled from two or more of the major credit repositories. Contrast with a Residential Mortgage Credit Report (RMCR) or a standard factual credit report.

Modification
Occasionally, a lender will agree to modify the terms of your mortgage without requiring you t refinance. If any changes are made, it is called a modification.

Mortgage
A legal document that pledges a property to the lender as security for payment of a debt. Instead of mortgages, some states use First Trust Deeds.

Mortgage Banker
For a more complete discussion of mortgage banker, see "Types of Lenders." A mortgage banker is generally assumed to originate and fund their

own loans, which are then sold on the secondary market, usually to Fannie Mae, Freddie Mac, or Ginnie Mae. However, firms rather loosely apply this term to themselves, whether they are true mortgage bankers or simply mortgage brokers or correspondents.

Mortgage Broker
A mortgage company that originates loans, then places those loans with a variety of other lending institutions with whom they usually have pre-established relationships.

Mortgagee
The lender in a mortgage agreement.

Mortgage Insurance (MI)
Insurance that covers the lender against some of the losses incurred as a result of a default on a home loan. Often mistakenly referred to as PMI, which is actually the name of one of the larger mortgage insurers. Mortgage insurance is usually required in one form or another on all loans that have a loan-to-value higher than eighty percent. Mortgages above 80% LTV that call themselves "No MI" are usually a made at a higher interest rate. Instead of the borrower paying the mortgage insurance premiums directly, they pay a higher interest rate to the lender, which then pays the mortgage insurance themselves. Also, FHA loans and certain first-time homebuyer programs require mortgage insurance regardless of the loan-to-value.

Mortgage Insurance Premium (MIP)
The amount paid by a mortgagor for mortgage insurance, either to a government agency such as the Federal Housing Administration (FHA) or to a private mortgage insurance (MI) company.

Mortgage Life and Disability Insurance
A type of term life insurance often bought by borrowers. The amount of coverage decreases as the principal balance declines. Some policies also cover the borrower in the event of disability. In the event that the borrower dies while the policy is in force, the debt is automatically satisfied by insurance proceeds. In the case of disability insurance, the insurance will make the mortgage payment for a specified amount of time during the disability. Be careful to read the terms of coverage, however, because often the coverage does not start immediately upon the disability, but after a specified period, sometime forty-five days.

Mortgagor
The borrower in a mortgage agreement.

Motivated Buyer
Any buyer with a strong circumstance or reason to buy.

Motivated seller
Any seller with a strong circumstance or reason to sell.

Multi-Dwelling Units
Properties that provide separate housing units for more than one family, although they secure only a single mortgage.

Multiple Listing Service (MLS)
A group of brokers joined together in a marketing organization for the purpose of pooling their respective listings. In exchange for a potentially larger audience of buyers, the brokers agree to share commissions. The listings are pooled by using a computerized network.

Negative Amortization
Some adjustable rate mortgages allow the interest rate to fluctuate independently of a required minimum payment. If a borrower makes the minimum payment it may not cover all of the interest that would normally be due at the current interest rate. In essence, the borrower is deferring the interest payment, which is why this is called "deferred interest." The deferred interest is added to the balance of the loan and the loan balance grows larger instead of smaller, which is called negative amortization.

Net Operating Income (NOI)
The annual income generated by an income-producing property after taking into account all income collected from operations, and deducting all expenses incurred from operations.

Net Worth
Assets minus total liabilities and debts.

No Cash Out Refinance
A refinance transaction which is not intended to put cash in the hand of the borrower. Instead, the new balance is calculated to cover the balance due on the current loan and any costs associated with obtaining the new mortgage. Often referred to as a "rate and term refinance."

No Cost Loan
Many lenders offer loans that you can obtain at "no cost." You should inquire whether this means there are no "lender" costs associated with the loan, or if it also covers the other costs you would normally have in a purchase or refinance transactions, such as title insurance, escrow fees, settlement fees, appraisal, recording fees, notary fees, and others. These are fees and costs which may be associated with buying a home or obtaining a loan, but not charged directly by the lender. Keep in mind that, like a "no-point" loan, the interest rate will be higher than if you obtain a loan that has costs associated with it.

Note
A legal document that obligates a borrower to repay a mortgage loan at a stated interest rate during a specified period of time.

Note Rate
The interest rate stated on a mortgage note.

No Points Loan
Almost all lenders offer loans at "no points." You will find the interest rate on a "no points" loan is approximately a quarter percent higher than on a loan where you pay one point.

Non-assumption Clause
A statement in a mortgage contract forbidding the assumption of the mortgage without the prior approval of the lender.

Noncompliance
Failure to comply or obey.

Non-Conforming Loan
A loan that does not meet the Freddie Mac or Fannie Mae standards.

Notary Public
One authorized to take acknowledgments of certain types of documents, such as deeds, contracts, and mortgages.

Notice of Default
A formal written notice to a borrower that a default has occurred and that legal action may be taken.

Obligations
Any debts requiring present or future payment.

Offer
An expression of willingness to purchase a property at a specified price.

Offeree
One who receives the offer. When the buyer makes an offer to the seller, the seller is an offeree.

Offeror
One who makes the offer. When the buyer makes an offer to the seller, the buyer is an offeror.

Option
The right to buy a property at a specific price within a specified time period.

Optionee
One who receives or purchases an option.

Optioner
One who gives or sells an option.

Option to Purchase
An agreement giving the right to buy a property at a specific price within a specific time period.

Oral Contract
A verbal agreement. Verbal agreements for the sale or use of real estate are normally unenforceable.

Original Principal Balance
The total amount of principal owed on a mortgage before any payments are made.

Origination Fee
On a government loan the loan origination fee is one percent of the loan amount, but additional points may be charged which are called "discount points." One-point equals one percent of the loan amount. On a conventional loan, the loan origination fee refers to the total number of points a borrower pays.

Owner Financing
A property purchase transaction in which the property seller provides all or part of the financing.

Owner Occupant
A tenant of a residence who also owns the property.

Owner of Record
The individual named on a deed that has been recorded at the county recorder's office.

Paper
A mortgage, deed of trust or land contract provided in lieu of cash.

Partial Payment
A payment that is not sufficient to cover the scheduled monthly payment on a mortgage loan.

Normally, a lender will not accept a partial payment, but in times of hardship you can make this request of the loan servicing collection department.

Payment Change Date
The date when a new monthly payment amount takes effect on an adjustable-rate mortgage (ARM) or a graduated-payment mortgage (GPM). Generally, the payment change date occurs in the month immediately after the interest rate adjustment date.

Periodic Payment Cap
For an adjustable-rate mortgage where the interest rate and the minimum payment amount fluctuate independently of one another, this is a limit on the amount that payments can increase or decrease during any one adjustment period.

Periodic Rate Cap
For an adjustable-rate mortgage, a limit on the amount that the interest rate can increase or decrease during any one adjustment period, regardless of how high or low the index might be.

Personal Property
Any property that is not real property.

PITI
This stands for principal, interest, taxes and insurance. If you have an "impounded" loan, then your monthly payment to the lender includes all

of these and probably includes mortgage insurance as well. If you do not have an impounded account, then the lender still calculates this amount and uses it as part of determining your debt-to-income ratio.

PITI Reserves
A cash amount that a borrower must have on hand after making a down payment and paying all closing costs for the purchase of a home. The principal, interest, taxes, and insurance (PITI) reserves must equal the amount that the borrower would have to pay for PITI for a predefined number of months.

Planned Unit Development (PUD)
A type of ownership where individuals actually own the building or unit they live in, but common areas are owned jointly with the other members of the development or association. Contrast with condominium, where an individual actually owns the airspace of his unit, but the buildings and common areas are owned jointly with the others in the development or association.

Plat
A plan or map of a specific land area.

Plat Book
A public record containing maps of land, showing the division of the land into streets, blocks, and lots and indicating the measurements of the individual parcels.

Point
A point is 1 percent of the amount of the mortgage.

Portfolio Loan
A loan held (not sold) by banks as an investment.

Power of Attorney
A legal document that authorizes another person to act on one's behalf. A power of attorney can grant complete authority or can be limited to certain acts and/or certain periods of time.

Pre-approval
A loosely used term which is generally taken to mean that a borrower has completed a loan application and provided debt, income, and savings documentation which an underwriter has reviewed and approved. A pre-approval is usually done at a certain loan amount and making assumptions about what the interest rate will actually be at the time the loan is actually made, as well as estimates for the amount that will be paid for property taxes, insurance and others. A pre-approval applies only to the borrower. Once a property is chosen, it must also meet the underwriting guidelines of the lender. Contrast with pre-qualification.

Prepayment
Any amount paid to reduce the principal balance of a loan before the due date. Payment in full on a mortgage that may result from a sale of the

property, the owner's decision to pay off the loan in full, or a foreclosure. In each case, prepayment means payment occurs before the loan has been fully amortized.

Prepayment Penalty
A fee that may be charged to a borrower who pays off a loan before it is due.

Pre-Qualification
This usually refers to the loan officer's written opinion of the ability of a borrower to qualify for a home loan, after the loan officer has made inquiries about debt, income, and savings. The information provided to the loan officer may have been presented verbally or in the form of documentation, and the loan officer may or may not have reviewed a credit report on the borrower.

Prime Rate
The interest rate that banks charge to their preferred customers. Changes in the prime rate are widely publicized in the news media and are used as the indexes in some adjustable rate mortgages, especially home equity lines of credit. Changes in the prime rate do not directly affect other types of mortgages, but the same factors that influence the prime rate also affect the interest rates of mortgage loans.

Principal
The amount borrowed or remaining unpaid. The part of the monthly payment that reduces the remaining balance of a mortgage.

Principal Balance
The outstanding balance of principal on a mortgage. The principal balance does not include interest or any other charges. See remaining balance.

Principal, Interest, Taxes, and Insurance (PITI)
The four components of a monthly mortgage payment on impounded loans. Principal refers to the part of the monthly payment that reduces the remaining balance of the mortgage. Interest is the fee charged for borrowing money. Taxes and insurance refer to the amounts that are paid into an escrow account each month for property taxes and mortgage and hazard insurance.

Private investor
Any non-institutionalized source of funding for a real estate transaction.

Private Mortgage Insurance (PMI, MIP)
Mortgage insurance that is provided by a private mortgage insurance company to protect lenders against loss if a borrower defaults. Most lenders generally require MI for a loan with a loan-to-value (LTV) percentage in excess of 80 percent.

Probate
Court process to establish the validity of the will of a de- ceased person. Also, the process by which an executor, personal representative or a court-appointed administrator manages and distributes a decedent's property.

Profit and Loss Statement (P&L)
An income statement that shows earnings, expenses, and net profit.

Pro Forma
Projected financial statements based on assumptions.

Promissory Note
A written promise to repay a specified amount over a specified period of time.

Prorate
To divide proportionately, so as to determine actual amounts owed by the buyer and seller at closing.

Prospectus
A document prepared to outline the terms and potential profitability of a real estate transaction, usually presented to private investors prior to their commitment to a real estate project.

Public Auction
A meeting in an announced public location to sell property to repay a mortgage that is in default.

Planned Unit Development (PUD)
A project or subdivision that includes common property that is owned and maintained by a homeowners' association for the benefit and use of the individual PUD unit owners.

Purchase Agreement
A written contract signed by the buyer and seller stating the terms and conditions under which a property will be sold.

Purchase Money Transaction
The acquisition of property through the payment of money or its equivalent.

Qualifying Ratios
Calculations that are used in determining whether a borrower can qualify for a mortgage. There are two ratios. The "top" or "front" ratio is a calculation of the borrower's monthly housing costs (principle, taxes, insurance, mortgage insurance, homeowner's association fees) as a percentage of monthly income. The "back" or "bottom" ratio includes housing costs as will as all other monthly debt.

Quiet Title (Action)
A court action to establish ownership of property.

Quitclaim Deed
A deed that transfers without warranty whatever interest or title a grantor may have at the time the conveyance is made.

Rate Lock
A commitment issued by a lender to a borrower or other mortgage originator guaranteeing a specified interest rate for a specified period of time at a specific cost.

Real Estate Agent
A person licensed to negotiate and transact the sale of real estate.

Real Estate Broker
A licensed individual who arranges the buying and selling of real estate for a fee. A broker usually owns his/her own real estate company or is in a management position.

Real Estate Settlement Procedures Act (RESPA)
A consumer protection law that requires lenders to give borrowers advance notice of closing costs.

Real Property
Land and appurtenances, including anything of a permanent nature such as structures, trees, minerals, and the interest, benefits, and inherent rights thereof.

Realtor®
A real estate agent, broker or an associate who holds active membership in a local real estate board that is affiliated with the National Association of Realtors.

Recorder
The public official who keeps records of transactions that affect real property in the area. Sometimes known as a "Registrar of Deeds" or "County Clerk."

Recording
The noting in the registrar's office of the details of a properly executed legal document, such as a deed, a mortgage note, a satisfaction of mortgage, or an extension of mortgage, thereby making it a part of the public record.

Recording Fees
Money paid to the lender for recording a home sale with the local authorities, thereby making it part of the public records.

Red-Lining
Illegal practice of discriminating based on geographic location when providing loans or insurance coverage.

Refinance Transaction
The process of paying off one loan with the proceeds from a new loan using the same property as security.

Remaining Balance
The amount of principal that has not yet been repaid. See principal balance.

Remaining Term
The original amortization term minus the number of payments that have been applied.

Rent Loss Insurance
Insurance that protects a landlord against loss of rent or rental value due to fire or other casualty that renders the leased premises unavailable for use and as a result of which the tenant is excused from paying rent.

Repayment Plan
An arrangement made to repay delinquent installments or advances.

Replacement Reserve Fund
A fund set aside for replacement of common property in a condominium, PUD, or cooperative project -- particularly that which has a short life expectancy, such as carpeting, furniture, etc.

Restrictive Covenants
Private restrictions limiting the use of real property. Restrictive covenants are created by deed and may "run with the land," binding all subsequent purchasers of the land, or may be "personal" and binding only between the original seller and buyer.

Revolving Debt
A credit arrangement, such as a credit card, that allows a customer to borrow against a preapproved line of credit when purchasing goods and services. The borrower is billed for the amount that is actually borrowed plus any interest due.

Return on Investment (ROI)
The income that an investment returns. Profit based on the funds spent to reach it.

Right of First Refusal
A provision in an agreement that requires the owner of a property to give another party the first opportunity to purchase or lease the property before he or she offers it for sale or lease to others.

Right of Ingress or Egress
The right to enter or leave designated premises.

Right of Survivorship
In joint tenancy, the right of survivors to acquire the interest of a deceased joint tenant.

Risk Tolerance
Your comfort level when assessing risk vs. reward. You can take steps to minimize risk in real estate investments.
- Risk Takers –Like speculative investment strategies with attractive potential.
- Moderate Risk Takers – Like speculative types of investments tempered with knowledge of

the market demands and application of good investment.

• Risk Averse – Like guaranteed results without risk and are very uncomfortable with taking chances.

Rollover Loan
A loan that is amortized over a long period of time (e.g. 30 years) but the interest rate is fixed for a short period (e.g. 5 years). The loan may be extended or rolled over, at the end of the shorter term, based on the terms of the loan.

Sale Leaseback
A technique in which a seller deeds property to a buyer for a consideration, and the buyer simultaneously leases the property back to the seller.

Second Mortgage
A mortgage that has a lien position subordinate to the first mortgage.

Secondary Market
The buying and selling of existing mortgages, usually as part of a "pool" of mortgages.

Section 1031
The section of the IRS code that deals with tax deferred exchanges of certain property. General rules for tax free exchanges are that the properties must be: exchanged, similar, and used for business or as an investment.

Section 8 Housing
Privately owned rental units participating in the low-income rental assistance program sponsored by HUD. Landlords receive subsidies on behalf of qualified low-income tenants, allowing the tenants to pay a limited proportion of their incomes toward the rent.

Secured Loan
A loan that is backed by collateral.

Security
The property that will be pledged as collateral for a loan.

Seller Carry Back
An agreement in which the owner of a property provides financing, often in combination with an assumable mortgage.

Servicer
An organization that collects principal and interest payments from borrowers and manages borrowers' escrow accounts. The servicer often services mortgages that have been purchased by an investor in the secondary mortgage market.

Servicing
The collection of mortgage payments from borrowers and related responsibilities of a loan servicer.

Settlement Statement
See HUD1 Settlement Statement

Simple Interest
Interest that is paid on the loan principal.

Sheriff's Deed
A deed given at the sheriff's sale in the foreclosure of a mortgage.

Single Family Residence (SFR)
A general term originally used to distinguish a house designed for use by one family from an apartment house. More recently, this term has also been used to distinguish a house with no common area from a planned development or condominium.

Special Warranty Deed
The grantor does not warrant against title defects arising from conditions that existed before he/she owned the property. The seller warrants that he/she has done nothing to impair title.

Subdivision
A housing development that is created by dividing a tract of land into individual lots for sale or lease.

Subordinate Financing
Any mortgage or other lien that has a priority that is lower than that of the first mortgage.

Substitution of Liability
A buyer's assumption of responsibility for an assumable loan.

Survey
A drawing or map showing the precise legal boundaries of a property, the location of improvements, easements, rights of way, encroachments, and other physical features.

Sweat Equity
Contribution to the construction or rehabilitation of a property in the form of labor or services rather than cash.

Tax Lien
A lien placed on a property for nonpayment of taxes

Tax Sale
Public sale of a property at an auction by a government authority as a result of non-payment of property taxes.

Tenancy in Common
As opposed to joint tenancy, when there are two or more individuals on title to a piece of property, this type of ownership does not pass ownership to the others in the event of death.

Third Party Origination
A process by which a lender uses another party to completely or partially originate, process,

underwrite, close, fund, or package the mortgages it plans to deliver to the secondary mortgage market.

Time is of the Essence
Legal phrase in a contract requiring that all references to specific dates and times in the contract be interpreted exactly.

Title
A legal document evidencing a person's right to or ownership of a property.

Title Company
A company that specializes in examining and insuring titles to real estate.

Title Insurance
Insurance that protects the lender (lender's policy) or the buyer (owner's policy) against loss arising from disputes over ownership of a property.

Title Report
A document indicating the current state of title. The report includes information on the current ownership, outstanding deeds of trust or mortgages, liens, easements, covenants, restrictions, and any defects.

Title Search
A check of the title records to ensure that the seller is the legal owner of the property and that there are no liens or other claims outstanding.

Tract
A parcel of land generally held for subdividing.

Transfer of Ownership
Any means by which the ownership of a property changes hands. Lenders consider all of the following situations to be a transfer of ownership: the purchase of a property "subject to" the mortgage, the assumption of the mortgage debt by the property purchaser, and any exchange of possession of the property under a land sales contract or any other land trust device.

Transfer Tax
State or local tax payable when title passes from one owner to another.

Treasury Index
An index that is used to determine interest rate changes for certain adjustable-rate mortgage (ARM) plans. It is based on the results of auctions that the U.S. Treasury holds for its Treasury bills and securities or is derived from the U.S. Treasury's daily yield curve, which is based on the closing market bid yields on actively traded Treasury securities in the over-the-counter market.

Trustee - A party who is given legal responsibility via a Deed of Trust to hold property in the best interest of or "for the benefit of" another. The trustee is one placed in a position of responsibility for another, a responsibility enforceable in a court of law.

Truth-in-Lending
A federal law that requires lenders to fully disclose, in writing, the terms and conditions of a mortgage, including the annual percentage rate (APR) and other charges.

Two Step Mortgage
An adjustable-rate mortgage (ARM) that has one interest rate for the first five or seven years of its mortgage term and a different interest rate for the remainder of the amortization term.

Two to Four Family Property
A property that consists of a structure that provides living space (dwelling units) for two to four families, although ownership of the structure is evidenced by a single deed.

Underwriting
The decision whether to make a loan to a potential home buyer based on credit, income, employment history, assets, etc.

Unencumbered Property
Real estate with free and clear title.

Unimproved Property
Land that has received no improvements.

VA Mortgage
A mortgage that is guaranteed by the Department of Veterans Affairs (VA).

Valuation
An estimation of value of a property, as determined by various factors.

Vested
Having the right to use a portion of a fund such as an individual retirement fund. For example, individuals who are 100 percent vested can withdraw all of the funds that are set-aside for them in a retirement fund. However, taxes may be due on any funds that are actually withdrawn.

Veterans Administration (VA)
An agency of the federal government that guarantees residential mortgages made to eligible veterans of the military services. The guarantee protects the lender against loss and thus encourages lenders to make mortgages to veterans.

Waiver
The voluntary renunciation, abandonment, or surrender of some claim, right, or privilege.

Warranty Deed
A deed, which guarantees the transfer of title from the seller to the buyer.

Wholesaling
Wholesaling real estate provides an opportunity for someone to build income with little to no capital or credit. A wholesaler puts property (normally distressed property) under contract and

assigns or resells the property to another investor. The investors a wholesaler sells to either use cash, lines of credit, or hard money loans. This allows quick closings on properties that sometimes need extensive repairs. Wholesaling does not require a real estate license. A license is not required to buy or sell any property that you have an equitable interest in. That interest can be a contractual interest (you have the property under contract) or you actually own or have title to the property.

Wraparound mortgage
A seller created mortgage that includes the remaining amount on a current mortgage AND any remaining amount to reach the agreed upon purchase price. The new mortgage "wraps around" the current mortgage. The seller is still responsible for the 1st mortgage. By making the needed monthly payments on the wrap around mortgage, the buyer will satisfy the terms of the mortgage held by the bank.

Yield spread
A rebate to a mortgage broker from the lending institution that purchases the loan on the open market. The yield spread is usually determined by the difference between the interest rate on the issued loan and the current prime rate.

Zoning
The process of determining what, if any, types of property may be placed in a particular land area. Common zoning distinctions include residential,

commercial, industrial, and agricultural. These zoning ordinances are normally enforced by the city or the county.

Real Estate Websites

"If you think math is hard try web design."
~ Pixxelznet ~

www.Auction.com

www.biggerpockets.com

www.blackmold.awardspace.com

www.Craigslist.com

www.Crimerates.com

www.Crimereports.com

www.Cyberhomes.com

www.Ebay.com

www.epa.gov/asbestos

www.epa.gov/lead

www.epa.gov/radon

www.fdic.gov

www.greatschools.org

www.gsa.gov

www.haslc.com

www.HomePath.com

www.HomeStagingResource.com

www.HomeSteps.com

www.HousingPredictor.com

www.Hubzu.com

www.HudHomeStore.com

www.justice.gov

www.NETROnline.com

www.nextstagefurniture.com

www.Pacer.gov

www.PropertyRadar.com
www.RealEstateABC.com

www.Realtor.com

www.RealtyTrac.com

www.REIblackbook.com

www.Recycler.com

www.resales.usda.gov

www.Schooldigger.com

www.selecthomestager.com

www.Stlouis-mo.gov

www.STLREIA.com

www.Treasury.gov

www.TruePeopleSearch.com

www.Trulia.com

www.Zillow.com

www.Zbuyer.com

Property Checklist

Property Checklist

Address _____

OUTSIDE:
Type of Exterior _____ Need Paint YES ___ NO ___
Rotted Wood YES ___ NO ___ Where _____
Roof Repair   YES ___ NO ___ Where _____ Layers ___
Lawn / Tree Service YES ___ NO ___ Where _____
Windows Replace YES ___ NO ___ Where _____
Gutters YES ___ NO ___ Any Other Outside Repairs Needed YES ___ NO ___
What? _____

FOUNDATION:
Type of Foundation _____ Need Work YES ___ NO ___
Clearance ___ " inches or more YES ___ NO ___ Type of Piers _____
Drainage Good YES ___ NO ___ Need Fill YES ___ NO ___ Where _____
Piers on PADS YES ___ NO ___ Are They Capped YES ___ NO ___
NOTES _____

ELECTRIC:
Breaker Box to CODE YES ___ NO ___ Hooked Up YES ___ NO ___
All Outlets Within 6FT. Of Water Equipped With GFCI YES ___ NO ___
How Old is Electrical System _____ Is Any Electrical Missing YES ___ NO ___
Wire Aluminum of Copper & What Shape is it _____
NOTES _____

PLUMBING / GAS:
Water Hooked Up YES ___ NO ___ Any Leaks YES ___ NO ___
If SO Where _____
Any Sewer Backing Up YES ___ NO ___ If so where _____
Is GAS Hooked Up YES ___ NO ___ Water Heater Electric ___ of Gas ___
Water Heater Properly Vented YES ___ NO ___ Water Heater Work YES ___ NO ___
Is The INLET hose to Water Heater Correct Type YES ___

INSIDE:
Need Painting YES ___ NO ___ Where _____
Need Sheet Rock YES ___ NO ___ Where _____
All Sinks Work Yes ___ NO ___ If Not What _____
Tubs work YES ___ NO ___ Notes _____ Toilets YES ___ NO ___ Notes _____
Carpet's Good YES ___ NO ___ Vinyl Good YES ___ NO ___
Should We Replace Any YES ___ NO ___ Where _____
NOTES _____

GARAGE:
Need Painting YES ___ NO ___ Need Roof YES ___ NO ___ Layers ___
Electricity YES ___ NO ___ Condition ___ Foundation Condition ___ 1 2 3 Cars
Sheet Rock YES ___ NO ___ Plumbing YES ___ NO ___ Water Supply YES ___ NO ___
NOTES _____

More Books written by: John Lee

Secrets of a Deal'ionaire

Creating Wealth One Small Deal at a Time

Foreword By *Robert Allen* – Multiple NY Times Best-selling author

"The reader cannot escape the conclusion the author knows his subject matter. I thought the government was the only one to make money out of taxes!" –William B. Beedie, Attorney

"In his new book, *Secrets of a Deal'ionaire*, John Lee teaches unique strategies for buying real estate with little or no money. *Secrets of a Deal'ionaire is* the 21st century's new book of *Nothing Down*." AJ Rassamni, author of Gain the Unfair Advantage

© HHLLC 2014, 2020. Secrets of a Deal'ionaire. Deal'ionaire OTC System Premier Signature Series. All Rights Reserved.

Another Groundbreaking Book by: John Lee

Landlord Pennies to Banker Dollars

Are you a landlord? Are you tired of the landlord myth of *Easy Passive Income*? Are you tired of *Toilets, Trash* and *Tenants*? Then this is for you.

With his revolutionary M.O.M. method, Lee shows you how to turn your hard-earned banker pennies into easy-collecting banker dollars.

A must read for all landlords and anyone who has ever thought of being a landlord.

© HHLLC 2014, 2020. Secrets of a Deal'ionaire. Deal'ionaire OTC System Premier Signature Series. All Rights Reserved.

Most Recent Credit Book by: John Lee

Secrets THOSE Credit Doctors Don't Want YOU to Know
Workbook Included

The information contained in this text has come from experience, i.e. blood, sweat, tears, trials and errors. It started off as a necessity from my own circumstances, turned into a lifetime quest to help others. There's a lack of good information when it comes to your financial and credit well-being. My intent is to provide you with good information that you will be able to apply to your own situation. By opening these pages, you are taking a giant step towards upgrading your life. Regardless of where you are currently there is always room for improvement. Our goal is to share experiences that will be beneficial to you.

© HHLLC 2014, 2020. Secrets of a Deal'ionaire. Deal'ionaire OTC System Premier Signature Series. All Rights Reserved.

What Others are Saying…

Ratings and Reviews

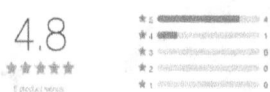

Knowledge is Power

Everything you need about getting your credit where you want it to be is in this book! Must have. ~ Steve D. ~

A really good way to understand your credit

I did not have an expectation. I wanted to have an open mind. The info in this book, which includes the workbook, helps you understand your credit in a better way. ~ David W. ~

Gift for my child

This is a gift for my daughter to help her understand how to best use credit to her advantage.
~ Regina O. ~

Knowledge that will last you a lifetime

Excellent book. ~Charles B.~

Very glad this book is available

I have been looking for information regarding ways to improve my credit score. Many thanks.
~ Milton T. ~

Other Books by: John Lee

Secrets Those Credit Doctors Don't Want You to Know
&
Accompanying Workbook

© HHLLC 2014, 2020. Secrets of a Deal'ionaire. Deal'ionaire OTC System Premier Signature Series. All Rights Reserved.

About the Author John Lee the Deal'ionaire

John R Lee has been investing in unconventional, unique real estate deals for over 25 years. He was a mortgage broker for many years and also has an extensive insurance background.

Lee's been around the block more than once. John's also written several best-selling books including, "Secrets of a Deal'ionaire" , "Landlord Pennies to Banker Dollars" and "Secrets THOSE Credit Doctors Don't Want YOU to Know."

Today, Lee focuses on education and stresses how important it is for you to succeed. One of the most important things John has learned is to get a mentor and jump-start your way to success.

As he always says, "There are two ways to do things, the easy way or the hard way. A mentor will get you there the easy way. The hard way is to spend twenty-five years learning it by yourself. Investing is a team-sport."

John is most famous for showing you how to turn $200 into $2,000 with about 2 hours' worth of work. By doing so you can spend more time with your loved ones and doing things you want to do, like he does.

The secrets and strategies John share are unique and priceless. He has simplified processes that can be very complicated.

© HHLLC 2014, 2020. Secrets of a Deal'ionaire. Deal'ionaire OTC System Premier Signature Series. All Rights Reserved

SECRETS TO START WHOLESALING REAL ESTATE TODAY

3 SIMPLE STEPS TO SCREAMING DEALS

© HHLLC 2014, 2020. Secrets of a Deal'ionaire. Deal'ionaire OTC System Premier Signature Series. All Rights Reserved.

To find out more about:

John Lee **and the Deal'ionaire's latest books and upcoming events, visit**

www.theDEALIONAIRE.com

You may also email John directly at

theDEALIONAIRE@gmail.com

© HHLLC 2014, 2020. Secrets of a Deal'ionaire. Deal'ionaire OTC System Premier Signature Series. All Rights Reserved.

www.ingramcontent.com/pod-product-compliance
Lightning Source LLC
Chambersburg PA
CBHW071355210526
45465CB00001B/100